Culture, politics, spirituality and practice:
A book of resistance and critical theory
for disturbing times

Culture, politics, spirituality and practice: A book of resistance and critical theory for disturbing times

A collection by
Makungu M Akinyela

Dulwich Centre Foundation
Adelaide, South Australia

ISBN: 978-1-7637156-5-3

Copyright © Makungu Akinyela 2025

This collection © Dulwich Centre Foundation 2025

Chapter 2 was originally published in *Journal of Systemic Therapies*, 24/1 (2005): 5–18. © 2005 JST Institute. Used by permission of JST Institute.

Chapter 9 was originally published as "Rethinking Afrocentricity: The foundation of a theory of critical Africentricity" in *Culture and difference: Critical perspectives on the bicultural experience in the United States* (edited by Antonia Darder, Praeger, 1995, pp. 21–39). Used by permission of Bloomsbury Publishing Plc.

Chapter 10 was originally published in *Claim no easy victories: The legacy of Amilcar Cabral* (edited by Firoze Manji & Bill Fletcher Jr., Daraja Press, 2013, pp. 445–452). Used with permission.

Dulwich Centre Foundation
Halifax St PO Box 7192
Adelaide Tarntanya
Kaurna Country, South Australia, 5000

www.dulwichcentre.com.au

Dulwich Centre Publications acknowledges the Traditional Owners of Country and pays respect to Elders past and present.

The views expressed in this publication are not necessarily those of the publisher. No part of this publication may be reproduced or transmitted by any process without the prior written permission of the publisher.

To Chinganji Akinyela

My lifelong friend, my wife and "ride or die" comrade, standing with me on the frontlines of the struggle for freedom for over 45 years. Thank you for your confidence in my work and my dreams.

To my Tyler, Wheaton and Thigpen ancestors

That great cloud of witnesses without whom I would not exist. Your resilience and defiance in the face of oppression has made me the person I am today. May this book express the best of who you hoped I'd be.

Contents

Preface — IX

Part one: Postcolonial therapy — 1

1. Decolonising our lives: Divining a postcolonial therapy — 5
2. Testimony of hope: African-centred praxis for therapeutic ends — 31
3. Decolonised counselling in a time of rising fascism — 51

Part two: Acknowledging our ancestors, healing our lives — 57

4. Standing together at the Door of Return — 61
5. Opening the Door of Return — 69
6. Spiritual accountability and balance: A story from the counselling room — 79
7. Connecting with ancestral struggle to strengthen resistance — 81

Part three: Thinking critically about culture — 85

8. Kujichagulia: Self-determination and the power of names — 89
9. Rethinking Afrocentricity: The foundation of a theory of critical Africentricity — 97
10. Cabral, Black liberation and cultural struggle — 123
11. Culture is the heartbeat of revolution — 131
12. Cultural resistance when the house is burning — 135

Part four: Education as freedom   139

13. Education as an experience of freedom:
    African-centred critical pedagogy and social justice   143

14. Valuing everyday resistance in Black family life:
    A story of critical pedagogy from the university of the streets   163

15. Fugitive pedagogies   171

Part five: Black religion, resistance and revolutionary spirituality   175

16. For future generations:
    Spiritual, religious and political practice   179

17. Let us march on   189

About the chapters   193

Abbreviations   197

Preface

The idea for this book emerged while I was travelling to Fort-de-France, Martinique, in August 2023 with my friends and colleagues Cheryl White, Serge Nyirinkwaya and David Denborough. These colleagues are dedicated internationalist allies for human rights and freedom. We were in Martinique to visit Frantz Fanon's birthplace and learn more about the context for the development of his ideas. While we were there, we watched a livestream of a memorial for Dr Mutulu Shakur taking place in Atlanta, Georgia. Dr Shakur, who was a dear comrade and friend of mine, was held for over 30 years as a political prisoner in multiple federal prisons around the United States. He was released only months before his death after a long struggle to free him from captivity. As we watched the online memorial together and discussed these histories and my life experiences, my colleagues began to encourage me to create a book that could gather in one place some of my diverse writings related to decolonising therapy, education as freedom, revolutionary spirituality and critical thinking about culture.

    Since our time together in Martinique, much has changed. Rising white supremacist nationalism, the re-election of Donald Trump as President of the United States, and increasing authoritarianism give new meaning to the ideas, stories, politics and histories conveyed in this book. Sharing it with readers now, in early 2025, represents one of many projects and responses to these profoundly disturbing times.

This book also includes the words of James Anani Amemasor, a Ghanian historian now at Rutgers University, who was also supposed to be with us in Martinique but was unable to obtain a visa in time. Cheryl, David and I first met James more than 20 years ago at Cape Coast Castle in Ghana. His words are included in these pages in relation to the theme of "acknowledging our ancestors, healing our lives".

This book represents partnerships across three continents: Africa, North America and Australia. It is a book of defiance and critical thinking for disturbing times. Each section includes recent reflections about how the themes in the earlier published works relate to contemporary resistance. I hope that this book can offer company in this time of crisis.

Makungu Akinyela
March 2025

Part one:
Postcolonial therapy

Postcolonial therapy

In the therapy room these days, it is rare to get far into a conversation without some acknowledgment of the day's craziness or a terrifying new development coming from Washington DC. Now more than ever, a decolonising therapy is necessary. This section includes two earlier papers in which I describe my efforts to develop a postcolonial approach to counselling that I refer to as testimony therapy. I have also included a more recent interview in which I explore the significance of decolonised counselling in a time of rising fascism and the importance of therapy playing a bridging role between personal experience and community action.

1.
Decolonising our lives:
Divining a postcolonial therapy

I am a therapist of African descent, born in the United States. I consult primarily with families of African descent. I believe that the emotional, relationship and mental health concerns that families present to me in consultation can be best understood within the social, cultural and historical context of resistance against racial domination in the United States. Those families who come to see me are commonly struggling with questions and issues that have their roots in slavery and Jim Crow segregation[1] as well as the current system of what I refer to as American racial colonialism.[2] While it is now over 30 years since the end of Jim Crow, and many of our people are no longer *legally* discriminated against, Eurocentric thinking, metaphors and dominant narratives continue to define relationships among Africans in America and between African and European Americans.

At the same time, the effects of colonialism and ongoing white race privilege continue to influence the worldview, practices and motivations of Africans in America. Various African thinkers throughout the diaspora have written about the experience of internalised colonialism or double consciousness (Du Bois, 1903/1989; Fanon, 1967). One of the key challenges for African therapists in the United States is to find ways of healing this double consciousness or internalised colonialism, ways that are grounded in the culture of our own people. As colonised people, our healing must come through self-determined action. The task for those of us from African traditions is therefore to take steps in generating and identifying culturally appropriate practices, processes and methods to heal our own. We are challenged to rescue, reconstruct and define therapeutic metaphors based on our own cultural and historical experiences. This process is what I refer to as the development of a postcolonial therapy. I use this term fully aware that it does not adequately reflect the lived experience of many Africans, Asians, Latinos or other Indigenous peoples either in the United States or in other parts of the world. Many people are still struggling with colonialism. It seems almost naive to speak of "postcoloniality" from this perspective. Perhaps it would be more accurate to speak of an "anti-colonial" therapy. This might more accurately capture the ideas of peoples at various stages of relationship with the colonial condition. Postcolonial is a term that I will use in this essay primarily for clarity to begin a dialogue with other therapists about the dynamics that define the work of African, Asian, Latin and other Indigenous therapists as we strive to shape therapies from within our own cultural contexts. At the same time, I hope to begin to explore those areas that are similar to, as well as different from, the poststructuralist/postmodern therapies.

My own practice is focused on defining an African-centred therapy that honours the history, experience and cultural knowledge of the descendants of enslaved Africans in the diaspora, and this paper seeks to map out some ground in this direction. First of all, it explores definitions of culture, for if we are to develop culturally appropriate practice, it seems crucial to have a clear notion of what we mean by culture itself. Secondly, this paper seeks to place the development of a postcolonial therapy for Africans in the United States within the broader context of the writing, politics and cultural practice of contemporary and historical Pan-African thought. Thirdly, this paper briefly considers some of the key experiences of life of African families in North America that need to be understood by any postcolonial therapeutic approach. Fourthly, this paper explores the relationship between postcolonial and poststructuralist approaches to therapy. And finally, this paper offers a number of key principles that I believe can shape the development of a postcolonial African-centred therapy.

What is culture? Critical African-centred theory and postcolonial therapy

In order to map out possible directions for postcolonial therapy, it seems important to examine first what it is that is meant by "culture". Some of the most relevant considerations relate to the work of African-centred and Afrocentric writers and thinkers.

Africans in North America as well as in other areas of the diaspora have for many years been at the forefront of developing, defining and defending African-centred and Afrocentric world views as counter-hegemonic responses to the ongoing tide of Europeanisation (often described as Westernisation) of the world's cultures and perspectives. Such important thinkers as Maulana Karenga (2002), Molefi Asante (1991), Marimba Ani (1994), Asa Hilliard (1996), Ngũgĩ wa Thiong'o (1986) and others have made important contributions in questioning Eurocentric thought and its effects on the day-to-day lives of African peoples.

They have articulated how current African life in the diaspora and on the continent is dominated by European ethics and values that shape social policy, spiritual life, and political and economic processes. They have also described how this impacts the day-to-day lives of Africans around the world. This is as true in the realm of the mental health and interpersonal relationships of Africans as in any other aspect of our lived experience. The emotional pain felt by Africans in family relationships and day-to-day personal social interaction is proportional to the cultural impact of the dominant Eurocentric narratives that define how we ought to live our lives.

On these matters, and many others, I find unity with the Afrocentric liberation intellectuals mentioned above.

Furthermore, I agree with Karenga (2002) that an important task of liberation for Africans is the rescue and reconstruction of African traditions, perspectives and worldview. Ani (1994) referred to this as the *Sankofa* process.

Some Afrocentric thinkers (Asante, 1991; Karenga, 2002) have argued for the idea of returning to classical African cultures as our source of Afrocentric knowledge. The most often referred to classical culture being that of Kemit (Ancient Egypt). There is little doubt among most African-centred writers that Kemit, and the ideas, spirituality and worldview derived from it, are highly significant to world African culture. Nevertheless, this recognition of Kemit's significance does not support the notion of classical cultural paradigms as sources of knowledge. In other writings (Akinyela, 1995; see Chapter 9) I have articulated my ideas about the development of African-centred critical theory in which I have raised theoretical concerns about attempts to codify the cultural past and to define so-called classical periods of African history. I argue that this practice is an imitation of Eurocentric models that define Ancient Greece as the classical paradigm for Western culture.

While agreeing wholeheartedly with the basic Afrocentric argument of the need to create a major shift in the hegemonic Eurocentric epistemology, I believe that focusing on the idea of returning to so-called *classical* African cultures runs the risk of dehistoricising culture and knowledge and reducing the complexities of African culture. There is a danger in understanding culture and knowledge as static and unchanging rather than as constantly changing and socially constructed.

Culture is not a static set of customs, formulas or traditions. To attempt to locate culture in specific customs, traditions and ways of thinking that are not allowed to change may actually lead to the death of culture. I agree with Fanon (1963) who wrote, "the desire to attach oneself to tradition or bring abandoned traditions to life again does not only mean going against the current of history but also opposing one's own people" (p. 224).

Fanon (1967) pointed out that efforts to codify traditions and place static value on reconstructing the past out of forgotten cultural practices in ways that do not consider current conditions and realities is in conflict with an understanding of cultural knowledge as ever changing and dynamic:

> Thus we see that the cultural problem as it sometimes exists in colonized countries runs the risk of giving rise to serious ambiguities … Culture is becoming more and more cut off from the events of today … It is true that the attitude of the native intellectual sometimes takes on the aspect of a cult or of a religion … He sets a high value on the customs, traditions, and the appearances of his people, but his inevitable painful experience only seems to be a banal search for exoticism. (Fanon, 1967, p. 217, 221)

Before I describe the ways in which critical African-centred theory offers alternative conceptualisations of culture, I need to make it clear that I believe that African cultural and spiritual traditions are a critical aspect of the ongoing liberation struggle of Africans around the world. I am not arguing for turning away from these traditions, far from it. I have witnessed and have great respect for the ways in which Indigenous peoples both here in the USA and in Australia are in the process of reclaiming cultural practices that have been disrupted by relatively recent acts of colonisation (from 150 to 500 years) and putting these to use in current contexts. In similar ways, Africans in North America continue to make links with and relate to ongoing African cultures on the continent and to engage with the healing ways that continue to be practiced there. Later in this paper I will describe how I see this as a vital part of developing postcolonial therapies.

What I am hoping to articulate here is the problematic nature of relating to culture as if it were monolithic, as if it ever existed in a *pure*, classical sense and as if our task now were to reach back and bring the ancient traditions *unchanged* into our lives in the 21st century. Fanon (1967) described how problematic it is to conduct a static search for a reconstruction of a "glorious past" and to limit definitions of what *is* African to what *was* African. History also teaches us that calls for returns to traditional culture, when they are devoid of ethical interest in the wellbeing of the common people, with attention paid to the real effects of social, economic and political stratification on all members of a particular culture, can be used to justify exploitation and oppression. Indeed, a range of leaders in some African countries such as Mobutu in Zaire, Amin in Uganda, Burnham in Guyana and the Duvaliers in Haiti have exploited and oppressed Africans all while supposedly promoting *traditional* African customs and cultures.

If, then, the reifying of certain cultural traditions is fraught with hazards, what are other options for conceptualising culture? Critical African-centred theory posits that cultural phenomena take their form in the dialectical tension that exists in the asymmetrical power relationships between groups and within groups. From this viewpoint, culture is constructed as the more powerful and the less powerful segments of society contend for positions of power and privilege. This means that any given culture is actually a complex of contentious and complimentary interactions between asymmetrical class, gender, religious, language, sexual and other social groups.

Viewed from this perspective, culture is in a constant dialectical process of construction and reconstruction. This notion suggests that there is really no homogenous national culture so much as systems of contending social groups within national or ethnic communities. It is the contention and complementarity between these groups that continually produces and reproduces culture.

It is the tendency of culture to adapt from and adapt to outside influences as well as to influence other cultures.

Culture is constructed in the constant process of dynamic change. The resulting material manifestations of cultural phenomena—for example the artistic, social and political expressions of groups and individuals—are acts of resistance and survival that assist and motivate cultural actors to make sense of and give meaning to their collective existence. At best, we can only identify cultural historical moments in any civilisation's development, as opposed to identifying classical paradigms that define a culture for all time.

Black people in the United States have not been passive objects of a process of de-Africanisation on the one hand and helpless victims of Americanisation on the other. The idea of contention and complementarity suggests that Black people have been active subjects in the process of Africanising the European culture that they encountered and reshaping their own African culture in relationship to the new cultural practices they found themselves relating to. Whatever religious, linguistic, familial or sociopolitical form was thrust upon them has been appropriated, internalised and Africanised into a new collective ethos. There is no need to seek "pure" classical African cultural forms to prove the Africanity of Blacks in the United States. There have never been such unchanging forms of culture even on the continent of Africa.

Critical African-centred theory posits the need for Africans to develop a collective liberatory consciousness as a necessary act against Eurocentric control of Africans. Both Malcom X (Perry, 1989) and Frantz Fanon (1963) focused on counter-hegemonic action as the source of liberatory consciousness. This is also the locus identified by critical African-centred theory, and I believe this can serve as the basis for a postcolonial therapy for Africans living in North America. There are ways of honouring the traditions of Africa while allowing for creativity and change. There are ways of identifying resistance traditions within the culture. In doing so, African-centred therapists can create a context for counter-hegemonic action within the therapy room and can offer alternative options for those who consult with us. Later in this paper I describe some of the key principles that can inform such a therapy.

A question that many might ask at this point is: How does this effort to define an African-centred, postcolonial therapy for Africans in North America relate to the remainder of the diaspora? It is my belief that the project of developing a postcolonial therapy for Africans in North America is an important aspect of the broader Pan-African project of decolonising African hearts, minds, spirits and countries.

The Pan-African project:
Decolonising African hearts, minds, spirits and countries

I have recently returned from a trip to Ghana in West Africa, a country that symbolises the Pan-African struggle against colonialism. Visiting Ghana placed me squarely in the path of African history. To visit the home of WEB Du Bois, who along with Marcus Garvey linked the struggles of African people in America to those on the continent, to walk around the memorial to President Nkrumah, the first president of a formerly colonised, now Independent African country, and to honour my ancestors by spending time in the slave dungeons on the Cape Coast (Amemasor et al., 2002; see Chapter 5), all powerfully reconnected me as an African to the history of my Motherland.

It was an inspiring experience, and a sobering one.

Visiting Africa also reminded me of the effects of colonialism on that continent. Colonialism still has its claws in Africa. As Fanon (1967) described, Africans on the continent, in the Americas, and elsewhere continue to have a struggle to see ourselves as culturally unique people and not just as poor imitations of Europeans. We still struggle against the imposition of the cultural images of Europe in our hearts and minds. In Ghana, in the back of almost every other taxicab there was a picture of a pale blond-haired blue-eyed Jesus staring out at me. This same image can be seen in many of the churches and homes of Black people in the United States. It is a sad thing that in the midst of one of the most powerfully spiritual places in the world, the images of deity, of God, for many Africans remain to this day European images.

There were also other poignant moments. For instance, on the night I was leaving Ghana, an airport bureaucrat commented that she thought I looked much nicer in my passport photograph. The photograph was taken prior to my current dreadlocks. She preferred my hair trimmed short and neat in the conservative style acceptable to Western culture, rather than in the long locks that for many people represent resistance against European aesthetics. These moments reminded me that the struggle to decolonise our minds is one shared by all people of African descent. It confirmed again for me that all of us Africans are on the same road, in the same struggle.

Overwhelmingly though, spending time in Ghana was inspiring because Ghana has always been central to the Pan-African vision. Towards the end of the 19th century, and throughout the 20th century, Pan-Africanism linked people of African descent in the diaspora (especially the Caribbean and North America) to those Africans on the continent. Writers such as WEB Du Bois from North America, Marcus Garvey from Jamaica and George Padmore from Trinidad led the way in creating the initial Pan-African consciousness. Kwame Nkrumah was also a key figure. He studied at Howard University, a historically Black university, where he interacted with other African intellectuals in North America, and then returned to Ghana to become a fighter for the liberation and the independence of his country. When Ghana became the first colonised African country to become independent, Nkrumah was its first Indigenous president.

Pan-Africanism was a key motivating philosophy behind the independence of Ghana. Nkrumah clearly articulated that the Ghanaian people were struggling not only for the independence of their country but for the independence and the freedom of all African people (Nkrumah, 1965). Once Ghana established independence, Nkrumah ensured that the country became a centre for worldwide Pan-African struggle. Ghana became a place that other key Pan-African leaders visited. Du Bois, Padmore and Fanon all spent time there, and in many ways, Ghana remains the spiritual centre of Pan-Africanism.

Spending time immersed in these histories reminded me that the task of developing ways of healing for our people is located in this broader political tradition. A significant element of the Pan-African project is to decolonise African culture and the African mind (Ngũgĩ wa Thiong'o, 1986). This includes our approaches to healing. The *Maafa*[3], the attempted destruction of Africa that took place through the enslavement and colonisation of African people, had profound material as well as spiritual ramifications. Africa and Africans lost wealth, land and the means to support themselves as a result of this holocaust. A part of the healing of this harm will come through reparations (Akinyela, 2002; Robinson, 2000), through acts of redressing injustice. But African people's souls, spirits and minds have also been harmed. As therapists, it is our responsibility to find ways to heal our people in these areas. This is the task for those of us who are exploring what it means to develop postcolonial therapies.

The Pan-African philosophy embraces the contributions of all people of African origin. Relating this to the therapeutic endeavour, this means that there are healing traditions on the African continent that can continue to be relevant and meaningful to all African people. Likewise, those of us living in the diaspora have developed our own forms of healing and resistance that, in turn, can positively influence those on the continent. There is a two-way process required here. As Africans in North America and the diaspora, we will continue to turn to Africa to engage with the cultural practices of the continent, and those on the continent will continue to turn to us in the diaspora for ideas and forms of healing that we are in the process of developing.

Experience of New Afrikan families

African-centred postcolonial therapy in the United States will be based on the history and experiences of Africans in North America (New Afrikans).[4] New Afrikan people share a particular history that includes surviving the transatlantic slave trade, slavery itself, Jim Crow segregation and currently ongoing racial colonisation. We are also linked to a collective history of resistance movements—abolitionists, the civil rights movements, and Pan-African and Black nationalist movements. Throughout this history, there are ancestors and inspiring figures to whom we as New Afrikan people are connected and from whom we draw strength. These include Nat Turner, Denmark Vesey, Harriet Tubman, Sojourner Truth, Queen Mother Audley Moore, Fannie Lou Hamer, Malcolm X and countless others. African-centred postcolonial therapy for New Afrikan people will be located in this history and these traditions.

There is also a range of "psychological" experiences common to New Afrikan people that are important to consider. Frantz Fanon (1967) articulated in some detail the psychology of oppressed peoples. In his short but inspiring lifetime, Fanon described that as the colonised person begins to master the language and ways of being of the coloniser, in the world of the colonisers, the colonised imagines themselves becoming more and more free. As they master the language and culture of the coloniser, the colonised person hopes to be seen as more and more human by the coloniser. At the same time, however, the colonised becomes more and more alienated from their own people. Others have also articulated this experience. WEB Du Bois (1903/1989) described this phenomenon as a *double consciousness,* in which all-too-commonly the colonised begin to judge their own behaviour, actions, looks and relationships by the standards of the colonisers. Fanon (1967) described that for the colonised, there is always a third force by whom we judge relationships and ourselves. It is never simply that we compare ourselves with people whom we meet; we always also judge ourselves and our relationships through European norms and values. In this way, the norms of the coloniser are in the middle of our lives and relationships. This has profound effects on how we relate to one another.

Not only is the coloniser in our own minds, but for many New Afrikan people, the effects of racial colonialism are also an everyday reality. Having an awareness of the effects of what we call everyday racism is critical to the development of a culturally appropriate therapy. It can be tiring for New Afrikan people to constantly face and deal with racist assumptions, actions, structures and practices. In this context, each small everyday cultural act becomes political.

The different ways in which people deal with this in families can be a source of strain or tension, and having an awareness of this realm of experience is critical in developing any culturally appropriate or postcolonial therapy for New Afrikan people.

Postcolonial therapy and poststructuralist therapeutic approaches/practices

The development of postcolonial therapeutic approaches will take place in relationship to other approaches to therapy and healing that are currently practiced in this country and in different parts of the world. There is much to be gained from thinking through the relationship between postcolonial and poststructural therapies. Just as the poststructuralist writers and therapists are determined to separate from the normative judgements of dominant Western culture, so too are we postcolonial therapists, but from a different position, with a different history and a different trajectory.

The work of poststructuralist therapists (White, 2001) seeks to question the professional knowledges of the helping disciplines and instead to honour, acknowledge and build on the healing knowledges of those who seek counselling. Their emphasis on metaphors of story and narrative is resonating with many different communities (Wingard & Lester, 2000).

As we are struggling to free ourselves from Eurocentric assumptions and prescriptions for life, it makes sense that there is an overlap with the ways in which some poststructuralist European thinkers and therapists are reconceptualising the world of therapy. It seems significant to engage with these poststructuralist practices while taking care to define for ourselves the commonalities and the points of departure. Where certain aspects of poststructuralist practice resonate strongly with us, let us ask why this is the case. Are there cultural, historical and social reasons? Which aspects of the poststructuralist approaches fit with our particular cultural project? How are the particular practices of healing linked to our own histories and ongoing practices of culture? How do we wish to engage with these practices in our own ways and our own contexts?

The following section focuses on four principles of poststructuralist therapies that I believe share common ground with an African-centred postcolonial approach to therapy. I have tried also to show that these four principles, when engaged with in a New Afrikan context, take on a different shape and meaning, and will continue to do so as we go about the process of developing our own forms of healing.

Four principles are discussed here:

- storytelling and witnessing—
  creating meaning through call and response

- interpretation of meaning—divining meaning

- a nonexpert stance—resisting the imposition of meaning

- alternative stories—building on testimonies of hope.

Storytelling and witnessing: Creating meaning through call and response

The emphasis on *story* as a key metaphor that informs narrative therapy (Morgan, 2000) is one that resonates strongly with African cultures both on the continent and in the diaspora. The telling of stories is a very significant part of New Afrikan culture and there are particular storytelling practices that are extremely relevant to therapeutic endeavours. Perhaps most relevant is the recognition within African and New Afrikan cultures of the complementary roles played by the storyteller and the witnesses. It is acknowledged that the story is only complete when there is both a teller and a witness to the story. In fact, it is this *call and response* interaction between the storyteller and the witnesses that actually *makes* the story and gives it meaning. The story is created through the process of the call and response. The meaning of the story is created in the dialectic or relationship of call and response, of storyteller and witness. In the USA, if you attend any Black church you are likely to see this process in action. Those leading the ceremony are consistently joined by the witnesses who sing, call out and respond in a variety of ways to co-create the rhythm and the meaning of the stories that are being told. Just as poststructuralist or narrative approaches to therapy are based on an acknowledgment that meaning and alternative stories are co-constructed in the process of therapeutic conversation (Morgan, 2000), and actively engage in reflecting processes in order to facilitate this (White, 2000), this metaphor of *call and response* can provide a framework for the role of the therapist within a postcolonial therapy for New Afrikans.

Interpretation of meaning: Divining meaning

The interpretation of texts and meaning, or hermeneutics, is a significant aspect of postmodern approaches to therapy (Parry & Doan, 1994). This tradition acknowledges that rather than any one "true" meaning existing in relation to any situation, the meaning is crafted and created through processes of interpretation. In poststructuralist therapy, this creates space for therapists and those consulting them to collaborate on making new meaning from the events of their lives.

In West African culture, there is a messenger between humans and the gods called Èsù or Elegba (Gates, 1991). In West African culture, Èsù/Elegba is the deity who mediates divinations. He is the one through whom we find/make meaning. In this African cultural practice, you divine to solve problems and interpret the world. In the European tradition, the word hermeneutics is derived from the mythology of the Greek god Hermes who was also the messenger of the gods. In the African tradition, this divination or interpretation occurs through a dialogue, through a conversation, through the telling of stories and acknowledging that every story carries multiple meanings. In this way, a postcolonial therapy for New Afrikan people will involve inviting those who consult therapists into a divination of meaning. Indeed, the process of therapy is one of divination. This is not a situation in which the therapist is the expert diviner, but both therapist and those who have come to therapy are engaged in a joint process of divining meaning and creating alternative meanings in relation to the events and stories of people's lives. In this way, the question of meaning is vitally important in the therapeutic endeavour.

Èsù/Elegba is also the keeper of crossroads, which in a number of West African cultures are a sacred space (Thompson, 1981). Crossroads represent the space between the spirit world and the material world. It's also a space in which decisions are made. In conceptualising therapy with New Afrikan families, this metaphor of crossroads has become important to me. When talking with families, and when meanings about events in their lives and relationships are being discussed/created, I am aware that in every conversation and relational interaction, decisions are being made that will either invite a turn towards preferred meanings or meanings that may lead them away from the directions in which they wish to head.

Thinking of a family as being at a crossroads, at a sacred place where decisions are being made, assists me in thinking through my role as a therapist. Just as Èsù/Elegba is the keeper of the crossroads, as therapists we have particular responsibilities in co-creating the meanings that are formed in the conversations we share.

A nonexpert stance: Resisting the imposition of meaning and creating a context for freedom

Poststructuralist therapists have made a clear shift away from positioning themselves as experts in relation to the lives of those who consult them (White, 1997). This is a significant departure from previous forms of family therapy and psychological approaches more generally. In developing postcolonial approaches to therapy, it is possible to link this work to what Paulo Freire wrote in relation to pedagogy (1990).

Freire described how any pedagogical experience can either be an experience of oppression or an experience of freedom. He then went on to explain the principles that underpin a pedagogy of freedom. In relation to therapy, an experience of oppression is one in which the therapist imposes *their* meaning, *their* interpretation, *their* "cure" on the person who has come for assistance. To assume that somehow as a therapist we can hold the secrets of the meaning of somebody else's life, and impose our interpretations on that life, can only serve to further colonise the minds and spirits of those seeking our help.

In order to create the experience of freedom in therapy, it is my responsibility as a therapist to offer a place as free as possible from imposed interpretations, either my own or that of the dominant culture. As described earlier, due to the influence of colonisation, all too often New Afrikan people live with Eurocentric judgements and values dominating their beliefs and dreams.

A key purpose of therapy is to create a space in which the members of the family can make their own meaning of events of their lives, in which they come to define their preferences for their relationships and lives, and where they can have the opportunity to be free of some of the prevalent Eurocentric judgements and values about their lives and themselves.

My expertise as a therapist is therefore not in being able to interpret or diagnose the lives of the families who consult me. It lies, instead, in being consciously aware of the ways in which the dominant Eurocentric culture can influence the lives of New Afrikan people and in creating a context in which families can come to their own understandings about their lives.

Alternative stories:
Testify'n and building on testimonies of hope

One of the significant contributions of narrative approaches to therapy has been the articulation of the significance of alternative stories and the methods by which these can become richly described and therefore more available (Morgan, 2000; White & Epston, 1990). Poststructuralist writers and anthropologists (Bruner, 1986; Geertz, 1986) have described the existence of multiple texts. There are the public texts (or dominant stories) that define individuals. These are the stories that *tell you* and that are supported by the broader power relations of the dominant culture. Then there are the counter-hegemonic texts or alternative stories from which you tell your own story.

In his book *Domination and the Arts of Resistance* (1990), James Scott described in some detail the "infra-politics" of life for people in colonised situations. He described the ways in which colonised people find means to resist and hold on to their humanity and dignity in spite of forces that are larger than them. These means of resistance are often pathologised by traditional therapy, and the people who practice them are labelled as *passive aggressive, resistant to change* or any number of other terms that reinforce the blaming of people as victims. From the context of postcolonial therapy, when the therapist can become curious about these acts of resistance and the meanings people give to them, opportunities for reclaiming dignity and humanity may be provided. I am interested in the counter-hegemonic stories that become available when we are aware of the infra-politics of everyday life as means of reclaiming dignity rather than as signs of pathology.

In my work with people of African descent, the tracing and development of counter-hegemonic stories occurs in a particular cultural and historical context. The stories of resistance that are built on are linked to and grounded in our people's traditions, cultural practices and history. Recognising this is important in the decolonising process.

In the New Afrikan spiritual tradition, to tell your story of how you have overcome, is called *testify'n*. When people begin to give their testimony, tell their story, the meaning and significance of the aspects of resistance or redemption often do not take shape until the story is told and shaped by the responses of witnesses. As described earlier, it is the process of call and response that builds on these testimonies of hope, or that thickens these testimonies.

New Afrikan people have rich traditions of testify'n. During slavery there were places called brush harbors where enslaved folk gathered to give testimony to one another and to have their reality witnessed and their survival acknowledged (Raboteau, 1978). Away from the eyes of white folks, these Africans could, for a short time at least, worship in the ways that they wished to and could give their testimony to those who would lovingly bear witness to it.

New Afrikan people also have long histories of redemptive song in which there is a dual acknowledgment of sorrow and hopefulness. This dual acknowledgment is the basis of the music that is known as "the blues". In terms of New Afrikan culture, there's always a kernel of hope in even the saddest of songs. That's the beauty of blues music and other New Afrikan musical traditions. WEB Du Bois wrote about the *sorrow songs* (1903/1989), the spirituals that were sung by enslaved Africans. These songs express profound sadness and longing, and yet there's always a kernel of hope or humour within them. There is always redemption written into the melody line. There is always a hidden testimony or a counter-hegemonic story to be heard, witnessed and built on. A significant part of postcolonial therapy, to my mind, is to create a space in which hidden testimonies can be told, in which people can give testimony to their lives, and through a process of call and response, this testimony can be thickened and made more meaningful.

Key principles for a postcolonial therapy for New Afrikan people

Having described a range of areas that I believe provide the broader context for the development of a postcolonial therapy for New Afrikan people, I would now like to summarise 10 principles that shape this endeavour. To create a postcolonial therapy for New Afrikan people, the challenge is to develop forms of healing and therapy that:

1. acknowledge the leadership and influence of our African predecessors in psychology and the social sciences, and that locate our work as following in their tradition; this includes acknowledging the healers and healing philosophies of Ancient Africa, the healing traditions of West Africa, as well as the psychological liberation work of Africans such as Frantz Fanon (1967), Amos Wilson (1991) and others

2. are based on a critical understanding that culture is never fixed nor homogenous, and instead is ever changing and the result of the contentious and complimentary relationships between differing groups in any given society at any given time

3. are centred in the history of New Afrikan people, including our history before enslavement, our resistance to and survival of the transatlantic slave trade and Jim Crow, and the links that all New Afrikan families have to the collective history of resistance movements

4. are centred in the experience of New Afrikan people including the effects of living with everyday racism and the effects of the colonisation of our own minds and spirits

5. invite counter-hegemonic cultural action based on the stories, history, experience, cultural practices and folk knowledges of New Afrikan people

6. continue to build Pan-African links and engage with current African traditional cultural healing practices on the continent, while also sharing with those on the continent our ongoing explorations which are also connected to African history and tradition

7. enable New Afrikan people to share the stories of their lives in a context free from the imposition of meaning, in which they can begin to identify and separate from Eurocentric assumptions, values and judgements and divine their own meanings about their lives

8. recognise and witness New Afrikan testimonies of hope, and utilise processes of call and response to thicken these testimonies

9. are our own—a central organising theme of African-centred postcolonial therapy is the idea of self-determined, independent cultural action; this therapy is developed from our experience, by us and in our own interest

10. are practical and effective—the therapy needs to work!

These are some of the key principles that I believe can inform the development of an African-centred postcolonial therapy. As we connect with African tradition and engage with some of the practices of life of our African ancestors and our brothers and sisters throughout the diaspora, we are not only returning to something old, we are creating something new.

What is my stance as an African-centred therapist towards those ideas and practices derived from European traditions? African-centred and other postcolonial therapists may and often do use some of the same therapeutic approaches in our work as our European colleagues.

However, it is certainly important that we are vigilant in making distinctions and clarifications about the origin of particular healing practices, and that we are constantly thoughtful about what would be necessary in a New Afrikan context to make such healing practices meaningful and appropriate. If we are grounded in our own history and culture, and if we are determining the direction of our work, when we engage with the healing practices of other cultures, we are not abandoning our ways; we are instead doing what our people have always done. We are reaching out and adapting and continually recreating cultural life. At the same time, it seems important to acknowledge that our engagement with these healing practices will also transform them (see section below on making genograms our own). In turn, this will influence the work of other cultures and communities in ways that we cannot yet imagine.

The very process of deliberately constructing a postcolonial therapy along the lines of the principles outlined above will generate something new. The process of decolonisation always does. The result of decolonisation is not to return to the state that existed prior to colonisation—that is never possible. The task is to free ourselves from the assumptions of the dominant culture, to place ourselves into the flow of our own culture and self-determined history in order to create our own ways of healing for New Afrikan families.

Creating pockets of freedom

It is my hope that in the process of developing postcolonial therapies for African, Asian, Latin and Indigenous peoples, we may contribute to the creation of pockets of freedom or "liberated territories". When struggles against colonial powers were taking place within Zimbabwe, Algeria and South Africa, pockets of land were won and referred to as liberated territories. In these liberated territories, people lived differently than they could in other spaces. In some liberation movements, these liberated territories have been specifically designated as places of healing for those involved in the ongoing struggle. These are places for people to go to rest and regather their energies before returning to the occupied territories to continue to struggle for freedom.

Similarly, in Brazil, further back in history during the days of enslavement, there were the *quilombos* (Schwartz, 1992). These were societies of Africans who escaped from enslavement and created communities that became beacons of hope and liberation for those still enslaved. In these societies, those who had been enslaved lived as free people and those who were running away from the slave territories were protected and supported. The *quilombos* were also used as bases from which expeditions were undertaken back to the enslaved areas to liberate others.

In no way do I wish to imply that therapeutic work in the United States of America at this time is the same as the struggles of those African people who fought for their freedom against slavery or struggled for liberation from colonial powers. Indeed, to make comparisons between the work that we do in a therapy room and struggles for political freedom is misleading and could be interpreted as arrogant. However, I think this metaphor of creating pockets of freedom is one that can be linked to my greatest hopes for an African-centred postcolonial therapy.

It is my hope that African-centred therapy could provide African individuals and families a space to talk about their lives, to make sense of their relationships, free from the interpretations and judgements of dominant Eurocentric culture. It is my hope that a postcolonial therapy could offer a "liberated territory" in which New Afrikan people could revalue their lives before heading back into a world that is so often hostile to the hopes and dreams of our people. It is also my hope that the development of a postcolonial therapy for New Afrikan people could play a small part in the broader overall struggle to decolonise our minds and spirits. By creating liberated cultural spaces, much the same way that we have created freedom schools, perhaps a genuinely postcolonial therapy can reinvigorate the aspirations of the New Afrikan people, and who knows where this could lead.

Making genograms our own

Within the field of family therapy, the genogram has been used in numerous ways (McGoldrick et al., 1999), some of which I believe are appropriate for New Afrikan families and others which are not. In developing an African-centred postcolonial therapy, it will be necessary to appraise the real effects of the use of any therapeutic practice and to develop ways to maximise their appropriateness for New Afrikan families.

One way in which the use of the genogram has been engaged with by New Afrikan therapists has been to acknowledge how New Afrikan families reach out and include nonbiological relationships within their families of choice. Throughout our history, as generations have been separated from one another, it has been a matter of survival to claim and remake families in whatever form would sustain our people.

The genogram has also been used differently by New Afrikan therapists in the location of family members' lives in the broader social and political context. For instance, in telling the story of a Black family in the south, in tracing the generations, it becomes critical to talk about the social, political and cultural conditions that those ancestors were living in, and to be curious about how they survived those conditions of life. It becomes a part of the process of developing genograms to wonder how one's mother or grandmother was able to get an education at a time when education for Black people was so hard to obtain. It becomes part of the process of developing genograms to trace the histories of resistance within any New

Afrikan family. The social context of our family's stories must accompany any exploration of their history.

In these ways, genograms can be used to engage with the stories of those who have come before us and to consider the legacies of particular values and practices that have been passed on through the generations. These are ways of honouring our heritage and our origins.

While the use of genograms was developed from European tradition, there are ways in which this aspect of family therapy practice is being reinterpreted and remade in our own image. As the concepts of family, heritage and history are of vital significance to New Afrikan people, engaging people in the construction and reconstruction of inclusive New Afrikan genograms is, I believe, one avenue for the honouring of our past.

Acknowledgment

I would like to acknowledge that the origins of this paper can be traced back to conversations shared with Rhea Almeida and Pila Hernandez.

Notes

1. Jim Crow was the name for the legal system of racial separation and structured exclusion and control of Black people from power in the American south. The Jim Crow laws of segregation were a model for the Apartheid system in South Africa. The civil rights and Black Power movements of the 1950s and 1960s in the United States were movements to dismantle the Jim Crow system.
2. Racial colonialism is the structured and systemic practice of economic, political, social and cultural privilege accrued by the collective Euro-American community that allows the exploitation of Black and other peoples for the benefit of the collective Euro-American cultural community. For example, the practice of redlining in the insurance and banking industries, which economically penalises residents of Black neighbourhoods because they live in certain geographical areas, allows those banks and insurance agencies to provide lower fees that benefit and effectively reward those who live in dominantly white areas. This system of rewards and punishment based on skin-colour/ethnicity has the same exploitative outcome of draining resources from Black population areas as the more familiar forms of colonialism.
3. *Maafa* is a Kiswahili term first introduced by Dona Marimba Richards (Marimba Ani) in her book *Let the Circle Be Unbroken* (Richards, 1994). Meaning "disaster", the word describes the human loss in what happened to us culturally, politically, economically, socially and spiritually with the European invasion of Africa. *Maafa* serves as a unique cultural description of our experience of genocide in much the way that the word Holocaust has come to be associated with the unique experience of Jews who suffered the genocide of Nazi domination.
4. Hereafter I will refer to "New Afrikans" as the cultural/national identification for Africans born in the United States (as distinct from Continental and other diaspora African national groups). This is my preferred term to identify Africans born in America and is one that is used by thousands of Africans born in the USA.

References

Akinyela, M. (1995). Rethinking Afrocentricity: The foundation of a theory of critical Africentricity. In A. Darder (Ed.) *Culture and difference: Critical perspectives on the bicultural experience in the United States* (pp. 21–39). Praeger.

Akinyela, M. (2002). Reparations: Repairing relationships and honouring ancestry. *International Journal of Narrative Therapy and Community Work*, (2), 45–49.

Amemasor, J. A., White, C., Akinyela, M., & Denborough, D. (2002). Opening the Door of Return: An interview with James Anani Amemasor. *International Journal of Narrative Therapy and Community Work*, (2), 60–63.

Ani, M. (1994). *Yurugu: An African centered critique of European cultural thought and behaviour*. Africa World Press.

Asante, M. K. (1991). The Afrocentric idea in education. *Journal of Negro Education*, 60(2), 170–180. https://doi.org/10.2307/2295608

Bruner, J. (1986). *Actual minds: Possible worlds*. Harvard University Press.

Du Bois, W. E. B. (1989). Of our spiritual strivings. In *The souls of Black folk* (pp. 7–14). Oxford. (Original work published 1903)

Fanon, F. (1963). *The wretched of the Earth*. Grove.

Fanon, F. (1967). *Black skin, white masks*. Grove.

Freire, P. (1990). *Pedagogy of the oppressed*. Continuum.

Gates, H. L. (1991). *The signifying monkey: A theory of African-American literary criticism*. Oxford University Press.

Geertz, C. (1986). Making experiences, authoring selves. In E. Bruner & V. Turner (Eds.), *The Anthropology of Experience* (pp. 373–379). University of Illinois Press.

Hilliard, A. G. (1996). *The Maroon within us: Selected essays on African American community socialization*. Black Classic Press.

Karenga, M. (2002). *Introduction to Black studies* (3rd edition). University of Sankore Press.

McGoldrick, M., Gerson, R., & Shellenberger, S. (1999). *Genograms: Assessment and interventions* (2nd edition). Norton.

Morgan, A. (2000). *What is narrative therapy? An easy-to-read introduction*. Dulwich Centre Publications.

Ngũgĩ wa Thiong'o. (1986). *Decolonizing the Mind: The politics of language in African literature*. Heinemann Press.

Nkrumah, K. (1965). *Neo-Colonialism: The last state of imperialism*. International Publishers.

Parry, A. & Doan, R.E. (1994). *Re-visions: Narrative therapy in the postmodern world*. Guilford.

Perry, B. (Ed.). (1989). *Malcolm X: The last speeches*. Pathfinder.

Raboteau, A. J. (1978). *Slave religion: The "invisible institution" in the American South*. Oxford University Press.

Richards, D. M. (1994). *Let the circle be unbroken: Implications of African spirituality in the diaspora*. Red Sea Press.

Robinson, R. (2000). *The debt: What America owes to Blacks*. Penguin.

Schwartz, S. B. (1992). *Slaves, peasants and rebels: Reconsidering Brazilian slavery*. University of Illinois Press.

Scott, J. C. (1990). *Domination and the arts of resistance: Hidden transcripts*. Yale University Press.

Thompson, R. F. (1981). *The four moments of the sun*. National Gallery of Art.

White, M. (1997). *Narratives of therapists' lives*. Dulwich Centre Publications.

White, M. (2000). Reflecting teamwork as definitional ceremony revisited In M. White (Ed.), *Reflections on Narrative Practice: Essays and interviews* (pp. 59–87). Dulwich Centre Publications.

White, M. (2001). Folk psychology and narrative practice. *Dulwich Centre Journal,* (2), 3–37.

White, M., & Epston, D. (1990). *Narrative means to therapeutic ends*. Norton.

Wilson, A. (1991). *Black on Black violence: The psychodynamics of Black self-annihilation in service of white domination*. Afrikan World Infosystems.

Wingard, B., & Lester, J. (2000). *Telling our stories in ways that make us stronger*. Dulwich Centre Publications.

2.
Testimony of hope:
African-centred praxis for therapeutic ends

The purpose of this essay is to articulate an approach to family therapy that speaks self-consciously from the cultural standpoint of African Americans and that challenges theoretical and cultural assumptions of universality in dominant Western therapeutic paradigms. This approach, called testimony therapy, is represented by a range of therapeutic practices grounded in the culture, history and experience of the African American community. Testimony therapy is communitarian[1]; that is, it emphasises the person within community. Testimony therapy is also social constructionist in its outlook, positing that people's ideas and practices are socially constructed and culturally mediated.

Testimony is a metaphor from the Black cultural/religious tradition of "testify'n". In the Black church tradition, testify'n is a ritual in which community members are invited to "give their testimony". In small Black churches, particularly in the rural south, an observer might even today be privileged to see churchgoers participate in a testify'n ritual. In such a ritual, an elder might begin humming or singing a song, perhaps a familiar "spiritual". After a few lines have been sung, someone might stand and wait patiently until the singing trails off. The one standing then begins to talk and tell a story. These stories in the ritual of testify'n begin with a recounting of personal or family problems experienced by the teller. As the person tells the story, they are encouraged at every sentence or so with a response of "amen" or "yes", or perhaps someone will affirm the teller with a "that's right". The storyteller who begins haltingly and is uncertain of the direction of the story seems to gain confidence as the responses become stronger and more frequent. A rhythm begins to build, and the story of doom and gloom begins to transform into a recounting of how, in spite of the problem, "with the Lord's help", things have got better. By this point, the witnesses have become full participants in the story, acknowledging their own certainty that the assessment of the good outcome is a correct one. By the end of the story, both the teller and the witnesses have woven their call and response to tell a community story. This community construction of a preferred story is a central idea guiding an understanding of testimony therapy.

The focus on storytelling situates testimony as a discursive therapy that shares similar ideas and practices with postmodern therapies, such as narrative therapy (Freedman & Combs, 1996; White & Epston, 1990) and solution-focused therapy (Berg & Hopwood, 1992; Miller & de Shazer, 2000), as well as with other culturally focused therapies, such as Just Therapy (Tamasese et al., 2003).

The interpretations of African American culture discussed here specifically rely on the shared cultural meanings that exist within the African American community. While I believe there are similar meanings understood by other African communities in the United States, as well as by West Indian and various Continental African communities, this article makes no claim for the universal application of testimony ideas and practices to all African peoples. Similarly, it must be noted that, as with all therapies, the therapist's and the client's class, regional background, gender, colour-caste and other contexts must be considered as testimony ideas are put into practice. These contexts shape the experiences for individual African Americans, precluding essentialist ideas of a monolithic culture. At the same time, an assumption of this article is that there is a common cultural ethos among African American people that has been shaped by a shared history of oppression and resistance to oppression. This ethos is the basis of the sense of "us-ness" and the common cultural meanings among most African Americans that transcend contexts of class, gender, education, region or colour-caste.

Why African-centred therapy?

This effort to define an Africentric[2] approach to therapy is much needed. In recent years, there have been various critiques and expansions in the field of family therapy, such as feminist critique of patriarchal ideas (Avis, 1986; Goodrich et al., 1988; Werner-Wilson, 1997), cultural critiques of the field (Di Nicola, 1997), and a revisioning of family therapy through a multicultural lens (McGoldrick, 1998). Perhaps most significantly, since the 1980s, family therapy has been challenged by postmodern and social constructionist theories of change (Anderson & Goolishian, 1988; Freedman & Combs, 1996; Gergen, 1998; Parry & Doan, 1994; White & Epston, 1990).

Articles about therapy with Black people are usually written from a Eurocentric standpoint within a broader context of multiculturalism, diversity and helping white therapists develop "cultural competency" (Bean et al., 2002; Becker & Liddle, 2001). Rarely do the writers privilege the knowledge indigenous to African American culture in the way, for example, that the feminist critique of family therapy privileges women's knowledge and experience as central to the development of feminist family therapy. This would be a primary objective in applying Africentric theory to family therapy. Boyd-Franklin's (2003) *Black Families in Therapy*, while not claiming an Africentric world view, was an early effort to accomplish this. Her groundbreaking book was for a long time the only text on family therapy written about Black people in the self-conscious voice of a Black therapist. Taking an African-centred standpoint asserts the agency of African Americans as self-determining subjects with their own resources for healing. The African-centred therapist looks to Indigenous practices, metaphors, spiritualities and understandings of mental health and wellness to set the pace for therapeutic work with families and individuals.

Principles of testimony therapy

Testimony therapy is grounded in the oral tradition of African American people. This oral tradition is evidenced in both the spoken word and the music (spirituals, blues, jazz, gospel, R&B and hip hop) of African Americans. Testify'n is the metaphor that describes the practice and the process of therapeutic work. For the purposes of this paper, metaphors are described as words or ideas that are used to symbolise an experience or concept. Through the description of one thing, another may be understood and the experience of that word or concept may be shared among people. In oral cultures, metaphor is a primary way that human beings communicate and discuss various experiences and concepts that are familiar in order to explain experiences and concepts that may not be familiar. Valuing the importance of orality in Black culture is a foundational principle of testimony therapy.

Testimony and spirituality

Testimony therapy honours the spiritual traditions of African Americans and recognises that, in the culture of Black people, the dichotomous line between secular and sacred is often non-existent. Testimony therapists understand spirituality as that experience of connectedness and relationship that is expressed in the customs, rituals, music and traditions of Black people. It is the tradition of "soul" that defines so much of African American culture, from soul food to soul music to soul theology. The spirituality of African Americans (Ephirim-Donkor, 1997; Paris, 1995) is also understood and expressed as an honouring of elders and ancestors and as a respect for the collective history and past of descendants of Africans enslaved in America. In a broader sense, the spirituality of African Americans of various classes and communities is expressed through metaphors that are invitations into African American understandings of the intangible. Some clients might speak of being in a "funk" if they are feeling depressed or of being in "the groove" if things are going well in their lives. A client who is agreeing with an explanation of something might let the therapist know that she is "feeling" the therapist, or, on arriving for a session, a client might declare, "The devil is trying to take my joy!" On the street, it is not unusual to see young Black men about to enjoy a cold beer pour a bit on the ground before taking the first sip as an offering to "the brothers who ain't here". Spirituality is widely expressed by Black people through belief in God and in various religious practices that may be Christian, Muslim, a traditional African religion or any number of traditions. While all African Americans will not respond in each of the ways provided as examples of spiritual expression or tradition, the unifying theme across class, gender and other contexts is the sense of unity based on the notion of *soul*, the power of the spoken word, the sustaining influence of rhythm and beat, and the healing power of ritual. All of these themes are understood within a context of community and belonging. When these themes or this communitarian context are disrupted, people may find themselves seeking the help of a family therapist or another type of healer.

Theoretical concepts key to testimony therapy

Testimony therapy is emotional

Testimony is emotional in that it creates space for the expression of grief, anger and joy that have been historically denied to African American people. This refers to both personal and collective grief, anger and joy, and to expressiveness that may often be deemed inappropriate in Eurocentric settings. Testimony therapy is concerned with fostering connections with family and community by utilising those culturally familiar processes that may help the therapist to elicit testimonies of hope. Kochman (1981), describing Black emotional force, argued that frequently the goal of African American cultural events is to revitalise energy through emotional and spiritual release. He described this emotional force by discussing three elements that he argued are necessary to achieving emotional spiritual release:

(1) a sufficiently powerful agent-stimulus to activate the emotional (spiritual) forces that the body has imprisoned, (2) a structure like song, dance, or drum that allows for the unrestricted expression of those forces that the agent-stimulus has aroused, and (3) a manner of participation that gives full value to the power of the agent-stimulus and to the individual's ability to receive and manipulate it. (Kochman, 1981, p. 108)

The Black church and other cultural settings have always provided this space of emotional freedom that allows Black people to find their healing by reconnecting with the deepest pain, as well as the deepest joy, that defines the personal and collective Black experience. The goal of the testimony therapist is to create the context for these three elements to be therapeutically helpful. According to Kochman (1981, p. 108), "the Black cultural pattern of *call and response* … integrates all three elements of stimulus, structure, and manner of participation (response) into a working relationship with one another". Testimony therapists work to create the space to include a range of emotions in therapy. They do this by being aware of conversational style and call-and-response rhythms in therapeutic conversations. Testimony therapists and their clients collaborate on constructing a healing testimony.

Testimony and the self

Most of us who have been trained in Western schools of therapy were taught that the goal of therapeutic work is somehow related to helping a client achieve or perfect individuation and movement towards self-realisation. Even within the systemic therapies, therapists were taught that the therapeutic goal was to help families avoid becoming enmeshed in each other's lives and to be able to have clearly defined boundaries and well-developed egos. All of these theories reflect what White (2001) critiqued as "internal-state" psychology. They assume that the self is a lone, isolated entity that exists somewhere inside the body of the person. These notions about the self as an isolated entity are taught as a fundamental part of Western philosophy: "I think, therefore I am" (Burnham & Feiser, 2001).

In discussing ideas of individualism with other colleagues of colour, I find that there is agreement that, despite the authority with which Western philosophy has been taught, we are often unable to reconcile it with our cultural experience of self, which is in *community*. For these therapists, personal identity moves between one's internal thoughts to relationships with extended kin and with the wider cultural ethnic community. This Africentric notion of self is reflected in the African philosophical axiom "I am, because we are; and since we are, therefore I am" (Mbiti, 1969, p. 106). This notion of personhood places emphasis on the communitarian and socially constructed self. Of course, this has far-reaching implications for the work of therapy guided by an African idea of mental wellness being expressed in social relationship, connectedness and belonging, rather than in individuation. The person in the context of African American culture is a "community of self " (Akbar, 1985), experienced as a collaboration of one's immediate and extended kin, the people of one's community of birth, and the wider community of African Americans and possibly Africans from other countries. This does not imply that African Americans have no sense of individual self. What it implies is that one's sense of individuality finds its greatest meaning and purpose in the context of community. For African people, community is the goal of life (Mbiti, 1969; Paris, 1995). Elia Mashai Tema (as cited in Paris, 1995) wrote:

> An African is never regarded as a loose entity to be dealt with strictly individually. His being is based on or coupled with that of others. Next to—or behind—or in front of him there is always someone through whom he is seen or with whom he is associated. The concepts of plurality and belonging to is always present, for example, a person is always viewed as: "Motho wa batho" (person of persons or belonging to persons). "Motho weso" (Our person or person that is ours). (Tema in Paris, 1995, p. 21)

Tema's description of the experience of the self can be heard in conversations by the frequent use of "us" and "we" as collective personal pronouns in the speech of Black people. From this perspective, all therapy with African Americans, whether with one person, a couple or a large family, is potentially relationship therapy. Any member of the community of self may be invited to participate in the healing conversation, either virtually or in reality, through questions to the client, such as, "What would your grandmother have said about your recent success in solving this problem?" or "What member of your family would be surprised at your recent success and who would not be surprised? Can you say why they would take these stands?" A testimony therapist may ask these sorts of questions, which include *absent* family members. The therapist must be fully aware that, though absent in body, these family members are always a part of the client and may be helpful to that person's healing.

Social construction of stories

Testimony therapy honours the community construction of story that is grounded in the Black oral tradition and that can be witnessed in various Black cultural environments. In these environments, the *way* one listens to a story is as important to the development of the story as the way the story is told. Likewise, in a testimony therapy session, the therapist does not listen passively as the client tells their story. The therapist recognises that the *way* they witness the story is important to the construction of the story. Both what is said and the verbal and nonverbal responses to what is said are important to setting the direction and meaning that the story takes. The way of listening and responding is more than *active listening*; it is an attunement to the cultural rhythms of conversation that mark the African American oral tradition.

Black conversation is often defined as much by the rhythm and beat or musicality that occurs between the speakers as by its content. By being open to witnessing and listening for thematic metaphors in the stories told by clients and by focusing on those "victorious moments" (narrative therapists call them "unique outcomes") that contradict stories of doom and gloom, testimony therapists intentionally participate in the construction of the story in collaboration with their clients. The therapist does this not by imposing their own plot lines or assumptions on to the story, but by remaining authentic as a witness and by being open and curious. Through their responses, both verbal and visual, the therapist encourages the storyteller to freely give their testimony.

Paying attention to the rhythm and the beat of the conversation

There is a spiritual aspect of testimony therapy partly expressed in the therapist's focus on the difficult-to-define notions of rhythm, beat, harmony and the energy of the work with the people who consult with us. It is in the rhythm, beat and energy of a conversation that a healing relationship of trust, respect and authenticity is built. This is maintained by verbal and bodily responses and contributions to the conversation, as well as by paying attention to the emotional energy, vocal tones and pace of the conversation. Conversations in the African American oral tradition may not be linear. They may seem to go in many directions at once. Anokye (2003), writing about oral tradition in the classroom, described this well when she wrote:

> Aspects of African American oral tradition are observable in African American student behavior. For instance, in story telling, African Americans render abstract observations about life, love, and people in the form of concrete narrative sequences that may seem to meander from the point and take on episodic frames. That is a style that causes problems with Anglo-American speakers who want to get to the point and be direct. In African American communication style we find the following: overt demonstration of sympathetic involvement through movement and sounds; a prescribed method for how the performer acts and how the audience reacts; total involvement of the participants; the tendency to personalize by incorporating personal pronouns and references to self … and use of active verbs coupled with adjectives and adverbs with potential for intensification. (Anokye, 2003, p. 74)

In therapeutic situations, when these elements are missing and European cultural styles of conversation dominate, Black clients may become disoriented or feel disconnected from the conversation. Clients may believe that the therapist is not really interested in them or that they are being "inauthentic". This does not mean that a therapist who does not usually speak in African American cadences or the grammar of African American vernacular English (Rickford & Rickford, 2000) must learn to do so. Paying attention to the rhythm and beat of a conversation requires self-awareness on the part of the therapist. Paying attention to *subjective* responses to clients' stories, though therapists have often been taught to suppress responses to clients' stories in a cloak of *objectivity*, can be a major step towards connecting with the rhythm and beat of the conversation. Listen to the rhythm of the conversation of the client. Is it slow or fast paced? If it were music, would it be blues or jazz, or perhaps hip hop? If you were to imagine that you and your clients were a music group, what instrument would you play to make the collective music? Perhaps you are the drummer, keeping the beat under the riffs and solos of the others. Perhaps you are on keyboards, moving in the dialogue between family members who are like brass and woodwind horns playing against each other. Or perhaps you are playing bass, setting a foundation for the rest of the group as individuals come forth to play solos and tell their part of the story. As you "demonstrate your sympathetic involvement" in the conversation, how might you pace your responses with the rhythm of the client? Does your body express connectedness to the story and does it invite further telling, or is it neutral and hard to read? The testimony therapist is self-aware of not only *what* is said in the response but also *how* they respond to the client.

Nurturing hopefulness by identifying victorious moments

Holding on to hope despite apparent circumstances of doom and gloom is an important aspect of the African American ethos. Hopefulness in the face of tragedy or crisis is a consistent theme in Black music from the spirituals and blues to hip hop. Much of this hopefulness is expressed by maintaining humour and a healthy sense of irony and paradox. Testimony therapists focus on listening for "victorious moments" that contradict the stories of defeat and powerlessness. Sometimes by further questioning about the moment, sometimes by verbal or body language responses in the rhythm of the conversation, these victorious moments are nurtured to place the doom and gloom story in a broader context of lived experience to provide new meanings for the testimony.

Nurturing hopefulness and listening for victorious moments requires skill development. Many therapists have been trained to listen for disorders and pathologies that can be reduced to a DSM diagnosis. Of course, the idea with this kind of listening is that if the therapist can find what is *wrong* with clients, they can then determine what will be required to fix them. Listening with the expectation of pathology or deficits usually guarantees that therapists will find them. It also consequently increases the probability that those practices, beliefs, intentions and aspirations that have helped people to survive and thrive in other periods of their lives will be overlooked. In the testimony tradition, therapists have learnt to *listen for the goodness in the middle of the mess* so that we can nurture that goodness through respectful, curious questioning about how it has occurred and how it has been helpful for the client. This is often a difficult task initially for therapists who have been trained to look for a diagnosis rather than to witness a testimony. It is also difficult when therapists have been trained to think of themselves as *experts* and of clients as victims who have no agency in their own lives. As therapists learn to respect clients as experts in their own lives with valuable keys to their own healing hidden away in their testimonies, stories are heard in new ways. Therapists also begin to respond to clients in ways that express a sense of hopefulness about the possibility of the client being able to move towards their preferred testimony. The following is an example of a therapeutic conversation between a testimony therapist and Muwata, a client consulting with him.

Case example

Muwata was a 50-year-old Black man who originally grew up in Detroit, Michigan, but who now lived in Atlanta, Georgia. He occasionally lived with his brother and the brother's wife when they were able to convince him to stay, but he more often chose to live on the streets of the city, or in shelters when it was cold. Muwata lived for over 25 years with a diagnosis of post-traumatic stress disorder (PTSD) and paranoid schizophrenia made after his return from military service and active combat in Vietnam in the early 1970s. He contacted the therapist through a social service charity after he decided that he wanted to talk to a Black man about his desire to be more proactive in his life and personal development. Over the years, he had received services from the Veterans Administration (VA). He spent time in the VA's psychiatric facilities, voluntarily and involuntarily. Muwata was politically and culturally astute, having belonged to several progressive political organisations over the years. The following transcript is a brief portion of a conversation in which Muwata described his journey to get help from the VA at a psychiatric hospital. He explained that he had not worked because of disgust with working conditions and bad treatment by supervisors.

Therapist: So you're saying that disgust starts say'n, "Muwata, you don't really want to do this. This is the same old set-up!" But there's something else that's say'n, "No, I got to handle this. I've got to deal with this [working]?" You feel more ready to do that now?

Muwata: Oh yeah.

Therapist: Why do you think you feel more ready now than before?

Muwata: Before, I got into a thing where the depression became very deep ... I had a dream [where] I was going through [a park] on a bicycle and the bicycle had a flat tire and I wasn't going anywhere. I think that dream was expressing to me where I was at in my life, and I became really depressed.

Therapist:	That was about three years ago?
Muwata:	Yeah.
Therapist:	So you felt—was it disgust again?
Muwata:	Disgust, despair, hopelessness …
Therapist:	But right now you don't feel that way?
Muwata:	No.
Therapist:	What have you been able to do to defeat disgust, despair and hopelessness? What have you been able to do to fight it back?
Muwata:	Well, I left the situation. I went to Tuskegee hospital to the psychiatric program …
Therapist:	You found it on your own?
Muwata:	A neighbour told me about it.
Therapist:	He told you about this hospital?
Muwata:	Right, right.
Therapist:	And it was helpful for you to go to this hospital?
Muwata:	To a degree.
Therapist:	How'd you get down there?
Muwata:	Greyhound [bus].
Therapist:	You caught the Greyhound? Who paid for it?
Muwata:	I did.

Therapist: So, you had this dream. You're like, despair, disgust, depression is attacking you, trying to convince you that life is hopeless. And there's someth'n in you that's fighting back against despair, disgust and depression and say'n, "Look, I'm gonna do something about this"?

Muwata: Umm-hmm. Yeah.

Therapist: And *you* got on the bus?

Muwata: Umm-hmm, Yeah [a look of surprise and realisation]. Oh yeah, *I* got on the bus. How about that! [laughs]

Therapist: [laughing] That's kinda deep.

Muwata: Yeah. But I also had reservations though [about going to the hospital]. I don't want people getting inside of my head. I mean this thing now [our conversation] is different. I don't want *the other* ... (let's flip it around on them and let them be the other). I don't want them getting inside my head. In essence, they're the ones that scrambled it up in the first place. I don't want to give them a *handle* on how to keep me in control.

Therapist: So, let me just recap. Three years ago, despair, disgust and depression tried to convince you that life was hopeless. Work ain't worth doing. You ain't going nowhere. You need to just give up. Those three *demons* were just trying to speak to you and get you to give up life, but there was somewhere in you that you found to resist—you got on the bus.

Reflection

Hopefully, in your imagination, you are able to hear the rhythms created by the call and response of this conversation. Of course, in print, it is very linear. In real time, in this conversation there are instances of crosstalk, give and take, call and response, and pauses and empty spaces that are all important to the construction of metaphorical meaning. This conversation is filled with metaphors that become places where Muwata and the therapist can meet for shared understanding of his life experience and its meaning to him. Getting on the bus becomes a metaphor for self-determination and agency in the face of victimisation and helplessness. The externalised problems of disgust, despair and depression, rather than being something that Muwata is or must remain, metaphorically become "little demons". This is a notion introduced by the therapist, who realises that often in the Black spiritual, religious tradition, problem practices and emotional experiences are externalised as manifestations of the *demonic*. Neither Muwata nor the therapist understood this as literal in the conversation, but it is a useful and culturally appropriate metaphor.

A recurrent theme in conversations among Black people is the expressed resistance to racist domination and manipulation shown when Muwata explained that he was hesitant about going to the psychiatric hospital even as he found his way there because he did not want "*the other*" (i.e., Euro-Americans) to "get inside his head". This metaphor, describing a stance of defiance and resistance, grows out of the healthy paranoia of Black people who have been victimised by centuries of unethical and genocidal experimentation and research on them by the medical and psychiatric establishments.

The four healing questions

A recent development in testimony therapy has been the introduction of the "four healing questions". This approach is both historically and culturally significant in that it reflects the centuries-old collaboration between Native American nations and Africans in the United States. For centuries, Black people in America and Native Americans have shared and exchanged cultural practices, sheltered and protected each other, and at times been part of the same communities as brothers and sisters. The four healing questions have come to testimony therapy from this tradition. Jackson (2002) introduced three healing questions to testimony therapy in her review of research by Pemina Yellowbird (2004). Jackson wrote of a conversation between herself and Yellowbird:

> A brief but powerful series of questions was offered by Pemina Yellowbird, author of *Wild Indians: The Untold Story of the Canton Asylum for Insane Indians* … As she and I discussed our respective history projects and ways to honor traditional methods of healing, Pemina noted that healers in her tradition offer three questions:
>
> 1. What happened to you?
>
> 2. How does what happened to you affect you now?
>
> 3. What do you need to heal? (Jackson, 2002, p. 25)

Jackson asks therapists to imagine the healing power of these words if they were a routine part of a mental health interview. This prodded the testimony therapy team to do just that sort of imagining. As the team thought about how these questions felt important, we also discussed what other questions might be useful. From that, an additional question, included as the third of the four questions, was developed that helps to uncover the victorious moments in the testimony. This question asks, "In spite of what happened to you, what gives you the strength to go on?" The fourth question then becomes, "What do you need to heal?"

The four questions derived from Native American and African American cultural experiences can be an extremely powerful therapeutic tool. They allow clients to tell their story and explore the impact of life events *now*. They invite clients to look for *goodness in the middle of the mess* and rely on clients' preferred testimony about their lives.

It is not claimed here that the four healing questions are a completely new modality of therapy. Other therapeutic modes may use similar questions. Certainly, the final question that asks the client to imagine what they need to heal may have a similarity to the "miracle question" of brief solution-focused therapy (Miller & Berg, 1995). The four healing questions are not a formula or a recipe to be used in every situation. Sometimes they are helpful and can be asked in one session just as you read them here. To assume a formula or to attempt to codify these questions would be to betray the spirit of spontaneity and improvisation inherent in the oral tradition of testimony therapy. Therapists are encouraged to experiment with these and similar questions that may facilitate the sharing of stories without retraumatising individuals.

Conclusion

This article has been an introduction to many of the ideas that have informed the development of testimony therapy. Testimony therapy is an African-centred approach to family therapy that is communitarian and social constructionist in its methodology. Testimony therapy offers both a critique of the dominant European cultural discourse on family therapy as it affects Black people and a corrective to dominant Western approaches to therapy. Testimony therapy is defined by metaphors of orality and musicality that are the basis of African American culture. This distinguishes it from Eurocentric therapies defined by metaphors of literacy and text that are the basis of Euro-American culture. While testimony therapy understands the therapeutic relationship, like all relationships, to be profoundly *political* (i.e., relationships always involve negotiations of power), it is not *ideological* or inflexible. In the best of African traditions, it is pragmatic and open to *what works* in therapy. The development of testimony therapy is a work in process. Like the best Black music and Black language, testimony therapy will be an ongoing creative transformation as others add their own innovations and creativity while holding on to core organising themes. The prospect of engaging in dialogues and exchanges of ideas with other therapists about African American culture and testimony therapy is welcomed.

Notes

[1] I use the word *communitarian* as a description of a key characteristic of testimony therapy, much as narrative therapists and other therapists describe their work as postmodern or deconstructionist. Among many of our colleagues of colour, there has been an argument that our work is not *postmodern* in that we are reclaiming the world view of our ancestors, which does not fall in the European timeline—though it perhaps coincidentally often resonates with European postmodern thinking. In a previous article (Akinyela, 2002; see Chapter 1), I struggled with the notion of *postcolonial* therapy. However, it was rightly pointed out by other therapists of colour that this term also limits us to the European-imposed experience of colonialism. At this juncture, *communitarian* seems to best describe how we situate our work.

[2] Throughout this article, I use the terms African-centred and Africentric interchangeably.

References

Akbar, N. (1985). *The community of self* (2nd ed.). Mind.

Akinyela, M. (2002). Decolonizing our lives: Divining a post-colonial therapy. *International Journal of Narrative Therapy and Community Work*, (2), 32–43.

Anderson, H., & Goolishian, H. (1988). Human systems as linguistic systems: Preliminary and evolving ideas about the implications for clinical theory. *Family Process, 27*(4), 371–393.

Anokye, A. D. (2003). A case for orality in the classroom. In A. D. Anokye & J. Brice-Finch (Eds.), *Get it together: Readings about African-American life* (pp. 72–75). Longman.

Avis, J. (1986). Feminist issues in family therapy. In F. Piercy & D. Sprenkle (Eds.), *Family therapy sourcebook* (pp. 213–242). Guilford.

Bean, R., Perry, B., & Bedell, T. (2002). Developing culturally competent marriage and family therapists: Treatment guidelines for non-African-American therapists working with African-American families. *Journal of Marital and Family Therapy, 28*(2), 153–164.

Becker, D., & Liddle, H. (2001). Family therapy with unmarried African-American mothers and their adolescents. *Family Process, 40*(4), 413–427.

Berg, I. K., & Hopwood, Y. (1992). Doing with very little: Brief treatment of the homeless substance abuser, *Journal of Independent Social Work, 5*(3/4), 109–20.

Boyd-Franklin, N. (2003). *Black families in therapy* (2nd ed.). Guilford.

Burnham, D., & Feiser, J. (2001). Rene Descartes (1596–1650). In J. Fieser & B. Dowden (Eds.), *The Internet Encyclopedia of Philosophy.* http://www.utm.edu/research/iep/d/descarte.htm#Meditation%202

Di Nicola, V. (1997). *A stranger in the family: Culture, families and therapy.* Norton.

Ephirim-Donkor, A. (1997). *African spirituality: On becoming ancestors.* Africa World Press.

Freedman, J., & Combs, G. (1996). *Narrative therapy: The social construction of preferred realities.* Norton.

Gergen, K. J. (1998). Constructionism and realism: How are we to go on? In I. Parks (Ed.), *Social constructionism, discourse, and realism* (pp. 147–156). Sage.

Goodrich, T., Rampage, C., Ellman, B., & Halstead, K. (1988). *Feminist family therapy: A case book*. Norton.

Jackson, V. (2002). In our own voice: African-American stories of oppression, survival, and recovery in mental health systems. *International Journal of Narrative Therapy and Community Work*, (2), 11–31.

Kochman, T. (1981). *Black and white styles in conflict*. University of Chicago Press.

Mbiti, J. S. (1969). *African religions and philosophy*. Heinemann.

McGoldrick, M. (1998). *Re-visioning family therapy: Race, culture, and gender in clinical practice*. Guilford.

Miller, S. D., & Berg, I. K. (1995). *The miracle method: A radically new approach to problem drinking*. Norton.

Miller, G., & de Shazer, S. (2000). Emotions in solution-focused therapy: A re-examination. *Family process, 39*(1), 5–23. http://dx.doi.org/10.1111/j.1545-5300.2000.39103.x

Paris, P. (1995). *The spirituality of African peoples: The search for a common moral discourse*. Fortress.

Parry, A., & Doan, R. E. (1994). *Story re-visions: Narrative therapy in the postmodern world*. Guilford.

Rickford, J., & Rickford, R. (2000). *Spoken soul: The story of black English*. Wiley.

Tamasese, K., Waldegrave, C., Tuhaka, F., & Campbell, W. (2003). *Just therapy—A journey: A collection of papers from the Just Therapy Team of New Zealand*. Dulwich Centre Publications.

Werner-Wilson, R. J. (1997). Is therapeutic alliance influenced by gender in marriage and family therapy? *Journal of Feminist Family Therapy, 9*, 3–16.

White, M. (2001). Folk psychology and narrative practice. *Dulwich Centre Journal*, (2), 18–23.

White, M., & Epston, D. (1990). *Narrative means to therapeutic ends*. Norton.

Yellowbird, P. (2004). *Wild Indians: Native perspectives on the Hiawatha Asylum for Insane Indians*. Center for Mental Health Services, https://power2u.org/wp-content/uploads/2017/01/NativePerspectivesPeminaYellowBird.pdf

3.
Decolonised counselling in a time of rising fascism

David Denborough: It's hard to find words to describe these profoundly disturbing times. As you are meeting with people for counselling or therapy conversations about what's going on in their personal and family lives, these conversations are now taking place in the context of rising authoritarianism and white supremacist movements. Why is a postcolonial therapy significant at this time to sustain people and their relationships? What are conversations in the counselling or testimony therapy room looking and sounding like at the moment?

Makungu Akinyela: Even before the 2024 Presidential elections (in which Donald Trump was re-elected), there had been a noticeable tension building in people's everyday conversations, on the street, in public. And in the therapy room, it is rare to get far into a conversation these days without some acknowledgment of the day's craziness or a terrifying new development coming from Washington DC through the news or on social media. Now more than ever, I think a decolonising therapy is necessary. First of all, to validate people's concerns and fears and to acknowledge that these are, indeed, extraordinarily difficult times. When you're feeling crazy, sometimes you need somebody to say, "No, you're not crazy. This is really happening. This is unusual. This is not something that we should get used to".

Can you say more about this element of naming within testimony therapy and why it is significant at this time.

Yeah. This is a crisis time. And first of all, it's important to validate to people that no, these are not normal times. It's also vital to name what's happening; for instance, to name the MAGA fascism that we are facing. That's not language that people in the United States are used to hearing, but it's important to have those conversations, to name the problem and discuss the problem and to acknowledge how fractured this can it makes us feel. At the moment, that also means acknowledging that we're afraid right now. And as a testimony therapist, I think it's important to acknowledge that it makes sense for us to be afraid or anxious now, because human beings feel fear and anxiety when their lives are in danger. And this is real. Our lives, as Black folk in this country, are in danger right now. This is a real existential crisis, particularly for colonised people. Naming this is important.

I'm trying to picture what this sounds and looks like in the counselling room. As a Black man, as a New Afrikan man, you are of the same people whose lives are being targeted. When people in your counselling room speak of their fear, when they trust you with their fear at this particular time, my guess is that you are responding to this fear in some particular way.

The way many of us have been trained to do therapy and to be therapists in North America is to place ourselves outside of the experience of the people who consult us—outside and oftentimes above them in an expert position. But this approach can often play out as seemingly inauthentic. Some Black folks might think, "You're not for real, you're being fake". But this shit is real for all of us, you know? So if someone is speaking about a disturbing event that we've just heard about in the news, I might respond with "This has been a hard day for me too". Acknowledging my own vulnerability, being transparent, being for real, not being fake is important. As a therapist, I'm doing this intentionally. Not because I'm falling apart or because I'm panicking, but I'm using honest words to connect and build relationship. I call this power of the word *nommo*, which is a term from the Dogon people of Mali. But of course, we have to go beyond these acknowledgments and find ways to create a transformative therapeutic experience for the folk who we're talking to.

Can you perhaps share a recent story from your therapy conversations to demonstrate this?

In this last week, there have been thousands of layoffs of workers from many federal government departments. The federal government has consistently been the major employer of Black people in this country for a long time (Pitts, 2011). Whether it's working for the postoffice, or working for different government agencies, there's now a lot of anxiety about whether or not people will be able to keep their jobs. This is an issue that has come up a number of times this week as people are anxious about the possibility of losing their jobs and the disruption this may also be causing in their relationships.

I'm thinking of one heterosexual couple where the woman is concerned that she may lose her job, and she is bringing in the most money to the family. In addition to this concern, she is also upset because her husband is doing what some Black men do: he is being real cool about it. This coolness is coming across as if he does not share her concern, and conflict is the result. But in talking to him, in front of her, it becomes clearer that it's not so much that he is not fearful about her losing her job, but he believes that it's really his job and his role to hold this kind of cool space and cool position, because for him, that's exerting a form of leadership. But it doesn't feel like leadership to this woman who is saying, "Damn, if I lose my job, I'm making the majority of money for both of us, what's going to happen to our house? How are we going to make our next car payment?" Our conversation together makes it clearer that they are both concerned, but they're responding in different ways.

Sometimes that cool Black masculinity, in which you got to look cool no matter what, can injure relationship. But I also want to acknowledge that this a part of culture—a culture formed in resistance to racism.

Our conversation also created a repositioning: Your husband is not the problem. Your wife is not the problem. This fascist takeover is the problem, and it can feel overwhelming, like drowning. These changes are having real impact on relationships, on the way people relate to each other. After this naming, we can then explore possible responses: What can we learn from your past experiences of conquering problems that could help you work together on this and not make each other the problem?

I really appreciate not only the significance of how these issues are named and linked to the current political climate, but also this re-engagement with history, turning to histories for possible ways forward. But what I'd like to ask you more about is how this conversation sought to bring people together to address problems. Is this also a significant theme at this time?

Yes, it is. Within the therapy room, I'm interested in seeking solutions other than "each individual got to get it together". I'm interested in seeking solutions of unity. Part of this involves inviting people to think about what past experiences they've had, where they've had success in challenging problems on the outside. And in this time of crisis, overcoming the threats we are facing is going to require the strengthening of community over individual interests.

That's a theme that our conversations are increasingly focused on. During this kind of "shock doctrine" (Klein, 2007) approach that's going on with this new MAGA fascist government, people can become more alienated than ever. So, in our therapy rooms, we focus on what the power of community is and getting reconnected with others.

When things were just low intensity warfare against us, it was easy for people to fall into the individualism of neoliberalism. But as Black folks, we have historically and culturally been communitarian people. As things have become more intense, I can almost feel a drive towards people looking for opportunities to be in community—a drive towards community for safety and security. Whether it's people going to church more often, or focusing more deliberately on their community organisations, or attending more social gatherings—these days in the therapy room we are talking a lot more about community.

It seems that in response to the crisis, people are increasingly looking outward and this is reflected in our therapeutic conversations. People are really seeing that looking and acting outwards is significant to their own wellbeing.

I'd really like to hear more about this. Are you explicitly asking more about these realms?

In these times we need a decolonising therapy that acknowledges solutions that go beyond just individualised solutions. So yes, I do ask explicitly. It usually starts with me asking about "How's it going for you this week? What's going on for you?" and I will then be listening carefully for whatever relationships they speak about. I think it's more important than ever to be able to sit back and see people within their networks and broader relationships and ask questions related to these; to help people weave strong bonds and connections that can be crucial at this time and in the future we are facing.

I might also hear how the person is feeling a sense of alienation from their job, or giving all this energy to people in their workplace who don't appreciate it or perhaps deserve it. Then I might ask questions that could invite a redirection of that energy, such as, "So what are you doing for your community?" And then I hear about what they are already doing or ways that they could make space to do more. These questions and conversations acknowledge for us the importance of being reconnected to community in these times.

So through these questions, it seems that the therapy conversations are acting as a bridge to other community actions?

Yes. And while that's always been true, I'm more conscious of it now. I'm more likely to ask about what's happening in your church or community organisation, or "Are you making any special connections at work?" I'm more conscious that in these times, therapy is about fostering unity, protection and possibilities for collective self-defence.

I really appreciate this understanding of counselling as weaving a sense of unity among people.

This crisis we are facing will require a strengthening of community over individual interests, so we will all need to play our part in this. There is one other theme that is emerging stronger than ever. I'm noticing that people are much more commonly referring to our ancestors' struggles and the strengths and cultural ties that helped them survive and that could possibly help us to survive. There's a different kind of a conversation taking place referring back to the legacies of our ancestors, our people.

That renewed engagement with ancestors and ancestry sounds like a really significant theme in relation to a decolonised counselling in this time of rising fascism. Perhaps we can return to that theme in our next conversation, because the next section of your book is "Acknowledging our ancestors, healing our lives".

References

Klein, N. (2007). *The shock doctrine: The rise of disaster capitalism.* Metropolitan.
Pitts, S. (2011). *Black workers and the public sector.* UC Berkeley Labor Center Research Brief. https://laborcenter.berkeley.edu/black-workers-and-the-public-sector/

Part two:
Acknowledging our ancestors, healing our lives

Acknowledging our ancestors, healing our lives

Now is a time that many of us are connecting with ancestors and ancestral struggle in ways that are strengthening our resistance. This section begins with a speech delivered at an International Narrative Therapy and Community Work Conference that took place at Spelman College in Atlanta. It is a speech I delivered on behalf of Ghanian historian James Anani Amemasor, whom I met on my first visit to the African continent. James acted as a historical guide for me, Vanessa Jackson, Cheryl White and David Denborough as we walked through Cape Coast Castle, a prison from which thousands of enslaved Africans were sent on ships to the Americas. The experience we had with James is described in Chapter 5, an interview called "Opening the Door of Return". I have then included a small story from the counselling room to convey how engagement with ancestry can provide healing to families. And finally, in Chapter 7, I discuss the significance of turning to ancestry at this particular time of struggle.

4.
Standing together at the Door of Return

James Anani Amemasor & Makungu Akinyela

A keynote address at the International Narrative Therapy and Community Work Conference held at Spelman College, Atlanta, Georgia, in 2002.

Makungu Akinyela

At its best, New Afrikan culture is based on honouring of elders and ancestors. When the dominant culture refuses to acknowledge in a meaningful way the realities of our ancestors' lives, and their hardships and their struggles and their resistance, and continues to construct systems that prevent us as New Afrikans from properly mourning and honouring our ancestors and their resistance to oppression, it brings shame and guilt on us.

To negate history is to dishonour our ancestors, which is to dishonour everything about us. What's more, when the injustices that affected our ancestors' lives remain unacknowledged, and when their stories of resistance remain unspoken, many Black people can be recruited into feeling ashamed of our ancestors.

There can be no more painful experience than this for people whose identity is so closely connected with family, kin network and ancestry. And so we continue to seek justice for those who come and for those who have come before us. We do so for many reasons. It's our duty, and it is what we owe those who lived in the past.

We also know that honouring ancestry is profoundly healing for us in the present and in the future. And so we do this not only for our ancestors and for ourselves but also for our children and our grandchildren. What the dominant culture refuses to acknowledge, we ourselves reclaim. There is considerable work now being done to reconstruct stories and write biographies of people who were enslaved.

There are also those who are working to find grave sites of enslaved people and to recognise those as sacred places. People are performing rituals at these sites and are reclaiming histories that are sources of pride. Today and every day, New Afrikans are acknowledging our ancestors and their sacrifices for us.

We will continue to seek reparations in relation to all they suffered and for our own struggles against domination. We will continue to reclaim, rescue and reconstruct history until the lives of our ancestors are properly acknowledged and our own lives are healed.

When we, Cheryl White and Vanessa Jackson and David Denborough and I, all met in Ghana, West Africa, to talk about this conference, we met a young man, 24 years old, I think, named James Anani Amemasor. And James took us on a tour of the Cape Coast Dungeon. He was the historian there.

We were so enthralled and fascinated by his connection to us that we talked about it, and we invited James to come here to talk to us here at this conference. The US Embassy would not allow him to have a visa to do that. But James sent us his talk because he was so excited about the idea of participating and we thought it would be important to include his voice.

In this piece, James writes to us.

James Amemasor

While I cannot be with you all in person today, I am with you in spirit. I'm so pleased that Dr Akinyela can read to you my speech as I wish to share with you some of my experiences of working as the education officer at the Cape Coast Castle here in Ghana. European contact with West Africa dates back to the 1440s. The Portuguese were the first to do so, reaching the shores of modern-day Ghana in 1471, and they began trading with the people.

This early European encounter with African culture did not assume any natural superiority over the African; hence, the established trade was a peaceful one. Due to trade rivalry between the Portuguese, the Spanish and the Dutch, quite a number of forts and lodges were built along the 500 kilometres of Ghana coastline.

Cape Coast Castle is one such building. It was originally built by renegade masons, carpenters and other African craftspeople. Little did the African artisans know that the forts they helped to put up would become theatres for an act that has no parallel in history. Soon after Columbus voyaged to the so-called New World in 1492, the Spaniards were taking West Africans across the Atlantic Ocean.

In the course of time, they opened a regular slave system, which eventually replaced the gold and ivory trade on the west coast of Africa. This new trade, the transatlantic slave trade, endured for the next three-and-a-half centuries. It involved the buying and transportation of Africans to the Americas to work on sugarcane, tobacco and rice farms.

The forts and lodges that were constructed initially to serve as warehouses consequently became the transit ports for the Africans to be enslaved in the Americas. Cape Coast Castle, where I work, became the most important fortress in the slave trade. At the peak of the trade in Africans, it served as the headquarters of the busiest European slave traders, the English, on the coast of Africa.

Today, Cape Coast Castle has been dedicated by UNESCO as a World Heritage Monument. A visit to its dungeons, its ruins and battlements reveals this land's history. It's my role as education officer to educate visitors and tourists, and to assist students and researchers. It's also my role to comfort and console pilgrims and returnees as they come to terms with what this building stands for.

Basically, I interpret the history to which this building is dedicated. This work offers me the chance to share with others the values that I hold dear. It also offers me the chance to share with others a history that is so sad, and yet, sharing it can also be inspiring. It is a history we cannot run away from.

My greatest moment at the castle is when I succeed in putting back smiles and hope on the faces of my visitors. The history of this castle is so important to us Africans because it helps us as a people to appreciate what happened in our part of the world and to plan our forward march. It is history that can assist us to understand what is happening today in our land.

It is history that can help us travel into the future as a united family with a common heritage and aspiration. And importantly, it is a history that helps us to understand and build on our connection with our kinsmen and women in the American diaspora.

Our work at the castle is done primarily through a guided tour. We walk through the castle dungeons and the castle rooms, the punishment cells, the Door of No Return, and then back into the castle. While the guided tour focuses on the tragic legacies of the slave trade and slavery, the museum exhibits and the video documentary include a range of other historical matters. These depict the pre-European cultural practices of the African and our history, European contact and colonisation, and Ghana's emergence to lead the continent in its struggle for freedom, realising its independence in 1957.

The exhibits also recognise the achievements of Africans and honour the New World that Africans have built in the Americas. We also discuss the role of Pan-African leaders Dr Kwame Nkrumah (first president of Ghana), Dr WEB Du Bois, George Padmore (of Trinidad), and many others who have made links between Ghana and the New World and have played their part in the reunion of the African family.

In this talk, though, I wish to concentrate mostly on the issue of the transatlantic slave trade. The principal means of capture were raids and wars. At the castles, the captives were exchanged for European manufactured goods, especially firearms. As more guns were brought for more captives, darkness fell upon the land as neighbours rose against neighbours.

The period of the slave trade was characterised by total insecurity, and this explains the African active role in the infamous trade. Although the transatlantic slave trade was institutionalised by European traders, some of us, the very unpatriotic sons of Africa, collaborated in this evil and were tainted by it.

Everyone wanted to protect their own skin and their own families. You and I know full well the ordeals the Africans went through in the Americas, and their achievements are all the more remarkable for this. But what of the survivors they left behind? The places and the people so savaged.

According to Professor Kwadwo Opoku-Agyemang in his *Cape Castle: A Collection of Poems* (1996), the slave trade was "an eclipse to whose effect we are still living". The African continent and its people were drained by the slave trade. The social customs, the political systems, the economies, the cultures were violently and irrevocably disrupted.

The slave trade and slavery are a wound sustained in the hearts of millions of people, and there is one place in the castle that most clearly symbolises this to me. The Door of No Return is the place that served as the point of final separation of the African family. It is the point where large numbers of African people lost contact with the continent.

It is the door through which Africans who had been captured walked into the ships that would take them into the Americas. The Door of No Return was where fathers and mothers, sons and daughters, uncles and aunts, brothers and sisters who had been captured in war and in raids were finally separated. They could not see each other again.

It is the place where people were separated from loved ones and from the land of Africa. It is a terribly powerful place, and we see some of our kinsmen and women from the diaspora weeping at this point. Whenever people stand there, they express their loss and their sorrow. The experience is humbling and moving.

Makungu Akinyela

And this is me talking: he's very right. When we walked out that door and walked back through it, y'all know I don't cry much, but I found myself sobbing. Because there was something he said, he said, "Welcome home", and that was important to me.

James Amemasor

The inscription "Door of Return", which is on the other side of the Door of No Return, received its official blessing on 1 August 1998. This was the day the first Emancipation Day was celebrated on the continent. Cape Coast Castle was one of the venues for the occasion. On this day, the mortal remains of two of the ancestors, Samuel Carson from Jamacia and Crystal from the US, were brought back to Ghana through the Door of Return. This was achieved through the collaboration of the immediate family and the government of Ghana. The remains of Samuel and Crystal were subsequently buried in Ghana. This was symbolic indeed. Even though those very ancestors might not necessarily have been taken from Ghana, it is enough that they have been brought back to the continent.

The act demonstrates not only the return of the ancestors through the same door they might have left to the New World, but also our sincere desire for reconciliation. It symbolises further the openness of the door to our sisters and brothers in the diaspora.

When we stand outside the castle, looking back at the Door of Return, I always tell my visitors to observe the movement of the sea. When you stand there at the Door of Return, you can see the waves moving towards the castle. So many people have been taken from Africa across those waves. But now the waves are bringing them back. Our brothers and sisters were once taken across the ocean, but they are now coming back through the same door.

The movement of the sea tells us a lot. When we re-enter the castle through the Door of Return, I welcome all my visitors, irrespective of where they are coming from. For our kinsmen and women from the Americas, I welcome them back to the continent. I say "Akwaaba", which means "You are welcome".

Our brothers and sisters from the diaspora often feel so happy when we welcome them back. For some time, they have not been on the continent and we've had some differences here and there. Our brothers and sisters in the diaspora sometimes point an accusatory finger at those of us on the continent, saying that we actually captured and sold them, and we cannot be left out of those responsibilities.

We do have a certain blame to share. The Door of Return acts as a reconciliation point between us. When we welcome them like this, and they feel they are a part of us, then it is possible for us to go about sharing peace, and even laughter, here and now. When other nationalities come here, like Europeans, I take them on the tour, and I tell them exactly what I tell my African brothers and sisters.

By the end of the tour, I try to talk a little about reconciliation, because I believe it's important. Without it, there will always be a gap between our people. There are other steps, too, that we have developed to make reconciliation and healing more possible. PANAFEST, the Pan-African Historical Theatre Festival, and Emancipation Day have been established to unite and reconcile the African people and friends of Africa.

PANAFEST as a cultural event offers us a unique opportunity to affirm our heritage as Africans, celebrate the heroism of our people, and investigate the horizon of our future. This is a biannual event. May I use this chance to appeal to all of you to attend this very important festival. Please come. At all these meetings, we place emphasis on the fact that our history, while very sad, is also a truth we cannot refrain from telling. To refrain from doing so would amount to running away from one's own shadow. The need for reconciliation cannot be overemphasised. Let us make each of us the centre of organisation for the unity and reconciliation we are gathering together for.

To end this talk, I would like to again mention the Door of Return. At the Door of Return, we emphasise the need for belonging to the continent. We symbolically embrace one another. We share tears of joy and a deep sense of belonging. The feelings at this point make the separated family a very complete one.

We then place high on our agenda the idea of redemption. We share ideas because we regard ourselves as a people with a common heritage. The Door of Return offers a reunion of the lost African family. The reunion is obviously a joyful one. Symbolically, we hold the doors open until all Africans can step forward, enter through the hallowed portals and come home at last.

Thank you.

Reference

Opoku-Agyemang, K. (1996). *Cape Coast Castle: A collection of poems*. Afram.

5.
Opening the Door of Return

This interview with James Anani Amemasor took place in Cape Coast Castle in Ghana, West Africa. Cape Coast Castle is one of the key fortresses used by the English for the purpose of slavery. Cheryl White, Makungu Akinyela and David Denborough were the interviewers.

To begin, can we ask you about your role here within this castle—what is it that you do here? And why do you feel this is important?

I work here at the Cape Coast Castle as the Museum and Monuments Education Officer. This job is very meaningful to me as it gives me the opportunity to express to others the values that I hold dear. It is my role to introduce our visitors to the history of this place, a history that we cannot run away from. Our history is very important to us. It helps us to appreciate what has happened in our country and enables us to then work out how we can forge ahead. Our history helps us to understand what is happening today in this land and assists us in travelling into the future.

Why are the particular histories of this place important?

Here at the Cape Coast Castle, we focus on and interpret the events of the transatlantic slave trade. This particular history is very important because it helps us to understand and build upon our connection with our brothers and sisters who are in the diaspora. It was through the transatlantic slave trade that many of our sisters and brothers came to live in the Americas, and this history is very important in bringing us together as a united people.

How do you go about this? How do you engage with these histories in ways that bring people together?

The history along this Cape Coast is most visible in the slave forts and castles which are scattered along the coastline. These buildings are monuments. They are physical legacies left behind by the slave traders and colonisers. These days they are also places to which people return. Our brothers and sisters in the diaspora come to visit these monuments to learn about what happened in the past and to learn about their roots. This castle is often their starting point. This castle, in which we are now sitting, was once a site where people were torn from one another. Now it is a site where people are coming together again.

It seemed to us that you took great care as to how you introduced us to the histories of this place. It seems you have thought about what stories to tell, and the video that was shown. Can you say a little about this?

When visitors come here, we try to be humble to them. We take people through the castle on the tour which we have developed, and then we show them a video documentary. This documentary describes the culture of our people before we had contact with Europe. It then goes on to show what happened after contact with Europe, the slave trade and colonisation, before describing our successful struggle for independence. Ghana was the first sub-Saharan African country to become independent. We are proud of this history, and we share it with our visitors.

And yet, there are still many ways in which our nation is struggling with neocolonialism. We have not yet achieved real independence either economically or in our own minds. Like other African people here on the continent and in the diaspora, we continue to struggle to obtain our freedom and independence. We discuss all of this here, and we also have a museum which describes the history of this country and the history of our brothers and sisters in the diaspora and their achievements.

Why do you think it is important for people in Ghana and Africans in the diaspora to come together?

In the first place, we share a common heritage, and we also have in common the blackness of our skin. Many of our kin in the diaspora are now turning back to the continent to claim their roots, and I believe this is very significant. This tradition has a history in Ghana. Many of our leaders, including Dr Nkrumah our first president, have emphasised the importance of making links between the people of Ghana and our sisters and brothers in the diaspora. When President Nkrumah obtained independence for Ghana, he invited people like WEB Du Bois, George Padmore and other key Pan-African thinkers to come and live here. These leaders were the link between the diaspora and the African continent. This was very successful, but it only went so far. We draw inspiration from these times, and we think that we have to bring Africans, wherever we find ourselves, together as a united family.

It seems that you are playing a unique part in the process. Every day you are immersed in these histories and are sharing the stories with others. What does it mean to you as a Ghanaian to be making these links?

During the slave trade here in Ghana we were all in a state of a stampede. There was no peace on the continent, only total insecurity. Families rose against families, neighbours against neighbours, tribes against tribes. The slave trade had terrible effects on those who were taken away, and it also left an indelible mark on Ghana. The traders took the strong and the skilled, and so the land was left depopulated and without many of its finest people. The stampede and violence of those times also led to political instability, which paved the way for colonialism. We are still dealing with the consequences of all of this here in Ghana. We are still trying to decolonise ourselves. It is ironic but we have also been uprooted from our histories. The work we do here is both for those of us here and also our brothers and sisters in the Americas. The slave trade affected us all. We share a history and so there is a need for us to come together.

The stories you tell here are very powerful and yet you walk within them every day. Each day, you walk through the dungeons, telling the stories, and it clearly has an effect on you each time that you do it. What makes it possible for you to do this each day and to do it in the loving way that you do?

I have been doing this work for six months now. It is always emotional and yet it has become part and parcel of me. No matter the situation, we cannot run away from our history. There is a need for somebody to always talk about this and to educate others. I have to do this. I try as much as possible to present the history in the way that it happened so that our visitors can learn about what happened here.

We'd like now to ask you about some of the particular aspects of the tour that you took us on. When you guided us through the slave dungeons, they were such desolate places through which many thousands upon thousands of people would have passed in terror and confusion and many others would have died. It was utterly heartbreaking to imagine people treating others in this way. It was also very hard to conceive how anyone survived the treatment they received here, let alone how they survived the middle passage to the Americas. You guided us through these dark cells until we came to the third dungeon where the shrine is in place. Can you tell us about this shrine?

The shrine in the final dungeon is dedicated to the god Nana Tabir. The local people of the Cape Coast worshipped this god in the image of a rock long before the construction of this castle. When the British settled here, the local people no longer had access to their god, so they moved the rock (which acts as shrine to Nana Tabir) out of the castle. It remained outside until 1974 when it was brought back to its original location. The shrine, which is now located in the final dungeon, serves an important purpose. It is there to inform our visitors that we Africans had our own religion long before we had contact with Europeans. The libation, or drink offering, which is poured whenever visitors enter the dungeon, proudly demonstrates our beliefs and reclaims the space as sacred.

The libation also serves to explain to visitors a little about the religious concept of African people. When the priest is about to perform the libation, he shows the offering to almighty God. He mentions the god's name and then he pours the libation. But the libation is not poured directly to God. Instead, it must be poured through the lesser beings. The religious concept of the African was that God created the universe, but that God is too pious to be contacted directly by humans. In the religious concept of the African, there are other spirits in the world which are closer to God than the human being. These spirits are believed to be in the images of rocks, trees, lagoons, rivers and lakes. So the libation is poured through these lesser beings and yet God is the ultimate receiver of the act.

Recently some professors of history in Europe have claimed that Africans did not have a history before Europeans arrived, and for that matter, that they did not even consider the idea of God. But these were just derogatory remarks. Africans have always had a concept of God, and the shrine and libation plays an important part in shedding the true light on African religious concepts.

For us, it was very significant that the shrine was there in the most desolate of places as it offered a sense of redemption. It was very important for me to witness the libation. To me (Makungu), as an African person living in the diaspora, it was affirming of our strength as Africans. When other Africans visit here, do they particularly appreciate the libation?

The vast majority, perhaps 90%, treasure it. But some of our visitors are Christians and they do not want to be a part of the libation. I am also a Christian, but I know that our forefathers had their own religion and whoever visits here I want to make sure that they also learn from our perspective and learn about the history of this land.

The other experience on the tour that we wanted to ask you about involved the Door of No Return. Can you speak about how you introduce visitors to that particular part of the Castle and what it is like for them?

The Door of No Return was the point where large numbers of African people lost contact with this continent. It is the door through which Africans who had been captured walked on to the ships that would take them to the Americas. The Door of No Return was where fathers and mothers, brothers and sisters who had been captured in wars and raids were finally separated. They could not see each other again. It is the place where people were separated from loved ones and from the land of Africa. It is a terribly powerful place and whenever people stand there, they express their emotions. For our sisters and brothers from the diaspora, this was the point where their ancestors lost contact with this continent, and for that reason it was known as the Door of No Return. It is a place where people express their loss and sorrow, and we see some of our kinsmen and women from the diaspora weeping at this point.

I then take people through the door itself, and we stand outside the castle, not far from where the ships would have once been. I then invite our visitors to look back at the door through which they have just come. Painted above the door on this side is now a small sign that says "The Door of Return".

In 1998, on 1 August, this door was relabelled the Door of Return. That was the day when the mortal remains of two African ancestors were brought back from the diaspora to the continent. One ancestor was from Jamaica and was called Crystal. The other was from the US, his name was Samuel Carson. Their families had brought these ancestors back to be buried on African soil. The remains were brought through what is now the Door of Return into the courtyard and a short but impressive ceremony was held. These ancestors were then taken into the country north of here, where there was once a slave market on the river that was called slave river. This is the place where the captives were washed for the last time before they were brought to the coast. The families reburied the ancestors there.

This event was powerfully symbolic in the sense that the ancestors were brought back to the continent. While these ancestors may not have necessarily been from Ghana, once they were brought to the continent and buried on the continent that is enough for us Africans. The ancestors were brought back and at the same time the Door of Return was opened for the descendants to come back and trace their roots.

This is clearly something that you feel is important. Can you tell us why?

When we stand outside the castle, looking back at the Door of Return, I always tell my visitors to observe the movement of the sea. When you stand there at the Door of Return, you can see the waves moving towards this place. So many people have been taken from Africa across those waves, but now the waves are bringing them back. Our brothers and sisters were once taken across the ocean, but they are now coming back through the same door. The movement of the sea tells us a lot.

When we re-enter the castle through the Door of Return, I welcome all my visitors irrespective of where they are coming from. For our kinsmen and women from the Americas, I welcome them back to the continent. I say, "Akwaaba", which means "you are welcome".

Our brothers and sisters from the diaspora often feel so happy when we welcome them back.

For some time they have not been on the continent and we have had some differences here and there. I have deduced that some of our brothers and sisters in the diaspora do not always feel so happy, so when we welcome them like this and they feel they are a part of us, then it is possible for us to go about sharing peace and even laughter here and now.

So the Door of Return is a very important place for us Africans of the continent and of the diaspora.

It must be significant for you, having just taken people through some of the terrible aspects of the histories, having been through the dungeons, for example, to then be in a place to welcome people back through the Door of Return. What is that like for you?

The Door of Return serves as a reconciliation point for the castle and for our histories. Our brothers and sisters in the diaspora sometimes point an accusatory finger at those of us on the continent, saying that we actually captured and sold them. And we cannot be left out. We do have a certain blame to share, but I always tell our sisters and brothers that the situation at that time was such that Africans who were on the continent had to fight to save their own skin.

To me, our histories are very sad. We cannot write that chapter out. It has happened. But we can try to come together and reconcile. When our kinsmen and women come back and walk through the same door through which their ancestors left, it is powerful for me and also for them. It is a point of reconciliation. It is a point where we state that we are all Africans—not just those of us who are on the continent, but wherever we find ourselves.

Do English and Dutch people also visit here to try to understand the histories that their ancestors were a part of? What is this like?

When other nationalities come here, like Europeans, I take them on the tour, and I tell them exactly what I tell my African brothers and sisters. By the end of the tour, I try to talk a little about reconciliation because I believe it is important. Without it there will always be a gap between our peoples.

Europeans do visit here. Sometimes it is rather unfortunate that I cannot see the impressions on their faces. When the people are of African descent, I can usually tell what is going on for them. This is not always true with Europeans. Only a few come and talk to me afterwards about the crime that happened here and their feelings about it. I know the majority deep down feel very sad about what happened here. I had some English and some Dutch people here recently who were taking the tour and who part-way through decided they could not continue. They said they were so ashamed of what their ancestors did here that they could not stay any longer. I believe there is a need for reconciliation with these people also.

Can I (David) say that it has been a very powerful experience for me as a white Australian to be here. I have some English ancestry, and I have felt shame, outrage and such sorrow at what occurred in this place. I also have an incredible appreciation and respect for the ways in which you are inviting us all to come to terms with these histories. The care with which you are doing this has been very moving to me.

And thank you also for giving me the opportunity to express in words what this place means to me. I have of course only been expressing my personal views. Thank you for letting people know about our Cape Coast Castle. We wish to act as the link between the past and the present. Whatever we have here we wish to extend to our visitors. So, for giving me this opportunity. I am also thankful.

While I (Makungu) teach African studies in the United States, and am of African descent, this is the first time I have been on the continent of Africa, and I am very glad that we came here. The ritual at the shrine, the libation and your welcome to us were all very important to me. I found myself sobbing as I came back through the Door of Return. They were good tears. When you welcomed us, I said to myself, I feel like I am home. At that point I felt more like myself than I have ever felt. That was very important to me and I really appreciated it.

Thank you so much.

6.
Spiritual accountability and balance: A story from the counselling room

Considerations of ancestry, spiritual accountability and balance are very relevant to counselling. This short story provides an example of this.

Within much of African spirituality, maintaining the balance and harmony in relationships and acknowledging connection and indebtedness are of fundamental importance. This is true in relationships between people and communities on earth and also between people and our ancestors. This spiritual accountability and balance can be important to good emotional and mental health. For example, the other day a woman came to see me who had been struggling with grieving a miscarriage. She spoke of a sense of "grieving everything" and "carrying the weight of everybody" on her shoulders. After talking together, we decided that we would engage in a ritual together in which she could release herself from feeling solely responsible for the lives of her friends and her relatives and her ancestors. Finally, we then turned to her dead baby, and I asked if she had poured a libation for her child. In African tradition, a libation is a drink offering—usually it is of water, but sometimes it is of wine, or even rum or whisky. The libation is an offering to ancestors, and it is generally poured into a plant or into the ground. This is a spiritual tradition followed by many Black folks around the world, including here in the USA.

Pouring a libation is to acknowledge the presence of your ancestors as a force in your life. This particular woman had not poured a libation for her child. She had not acknowledged the baby as linked to her in an ancestral way, or even acknowledged the child's humanity and importance to her, even though now she was caught in a cycle of mourning for the child's loss. And so we went outside and poured a libation for the baby. She called the child's name, expressed her love and identified herself as the child's mother. She then acknowledged the baby, its death and its ongoing presence in her life in a spiritual form. When she went home, she engaged in a similar ritual with her husband. Together they acknowledged the child's place in an ancestral chain.

This ritual is about restoring balance and harmony in ancestral relationships. Pouring a libation is a ritual of acknowledging the debt that we owe to our ancestors. It is offering acknowledgment that the presence of our ancestors gives us support, strength and guidance. Fundamentally, performing this ritual is about maintaining the reciprocity of relationships between the living and the dead.

7.
Connecting with ancestral struggle to strengthen resistance

David Denborough: I find it very moving to read those pieces by you and James and to recall our time in Ghana. As you and your community now face the consequences of an authoritarian movement that is deliberating turning back time in many ways, including evoking white supremacist times and Apartheid South Africa, are there particular ways in which your relationships with and honouring of ancestors are even more important than ever?

Makungu Akinyela: Now, in the midst of these crisis times, I am a part of many more conversations in which we are referring to our ancestors' struggles and strength, and an increased recognition of lessons learnt from our ancestors. I also hear more conversations about the cultural ties that helped our ancestors to survive, and explorations about how these could possibly help us to survive now and in the years to come. These sorts of conversations are much more prevalent now and they seem really significant. This is not the first time our people have faced an existential threat. It seems a moment when we are drawing on histories of ancestral struggle to prepare ourselves for what is to come. To prepare ourselves for our resistance.

This seems a different sort of reunion with ancestry than the one that you and James discussed, but it seems related and just as powerful. Are there particular learnings from ancestors who endured and survived the horrors of slavery and Jim Crow that you are drawing on now?

There are many things. During this time, there seems a harkening recognition of our ancestors' spiritual practices. Whether they were practitioners of traditional African religions or Christians or Muslims, we know that a part of the strength of our ancestors was their reliance on the spirit of the creator. I think in this crisis time, our people are broadening our sense of the spiritual and this very much includes a reconnection with ancestry.

Are there particular rituals and/or rememberings you are calling on both individually and collectively?

Yes, there certainly are spiritual rituals, but your question makes me think of a different sort of ritual that we are in the midst of right now. We are moving right now towards the end of Black History Month. This ritual began as a week set aside by Dr Carter G Woodson and the Association of Negro Life and History, now called the Association for the Study of African American Life and History, to combat what he called the physical and intellectual violence being waged against Black people at that time through the education system. That was in 1926. Now, each year, a month is set aside for Black History Month. This year, with the attacks on equity in education through the US Department of Education, as well as other attacks from various federal departments on the full access to inclusion and power, the celebration of Black History Month as a defence once again against physical and intellectual violence has been more necessary than ever. Joining in telling and retelling histories of struggle and honouring key figures of this struggle through song, ritual and scholarship has been significant to me and many others. In many ways, Black History Month is a collective ritual that involves connecting with and honouring ancestors and our people's struggle. I've never been more grateful for Black History Month than I have this year.

I have just one more question for now. As we are speaking, I've been thinking about your more immediate ancestors, thinking about what your grandparents lived through for instance. Is there anything that you are drawing from them, learning from them, honouring of them in this moment?

Thinking about my own ancestors is really important to me. I've created a huge genogram that I look at sometimes. I particularly turn to my ancestry on my father's side, my knowledge of which starts with my great grandparents who were enslaved people. Their survival always gives me inspiration. While on my mother's side, we know our maternal ancestors were Yoruba and probably came to this continent through New Orleans.

Engaging with ancestral histories can be complex can't it: multiple storylines and for many people also multiple family and cultural lines. It can also be complex thinking about more immediate ancestors. What does honouring more immediate ancestors mean to you?

When I think about immediate ancestors, I think about my grandfather, my grandmother and my father in particular, who all were activists in Mississippi. I learnt many of the most important lessons of my life by seeing them actively responding to injustices. So, too, watching my mother, who is not an ancestor yet, but who is an elder and was also an activist in Mississippi and always a strong fighter for women. When I think of them, I always feel like I've come from a strong start, with strong roots. I draw a sense of pride from that legacy and those traditions from which I come. But that history also brings responsibilities that can feel heavy at times. There are times when it's as if they are speaking to me: "So what are you going to do?" This is one of those times.

I know you are taking many different sorts of action at this time: as healer within testimony therapy rooms, as community organiser as part of grassroots movements, as family man, as well as teacher and as writer. I'd be interested to know more about the legacies from your ancestors that you are drawing on in each of these realms. Perhaps we can talk more about that sometime. Now though, this book is going to take a different turn, towards the importance of critical thinking about culture and the significance of cultural struggle.

Part three:
Thinking critically about culture

Thinking critically about culture

This section contains five diverse pieces, all of which seek to think critically about culture. There is an interview conducted in Martinique exploring the significance of the power of names; an academic paper rethinking Afrocentricity; a paper, "Cabral, Black Liberation and Cultural Struggle", written just after Barack Obama had been elected for a second term; a speech for the National Malcolm X Assassination Commemoration. The section concludes with a recent interview that explores the relevance of cultural resistance at this time of increasing authoritarianism. Now, and always, our culture is a heartbeat, a shield and a weapon.

8.
Kujichagulia:
Self-determination and the power of names

David Denborough: Can we start by talking about your name, Makungu Akinyela? I know that for you and also your partner, Chinganji Akinyela, taking these names has been powerfully significant. In narrative practice, we believe that people having the power to name their experience and to name problems in their own words and terms is political, but in the context of Black Power movements, your beings were renamed as part of political and personal liberation struggle. This seems really powerful, spiritually and politically. Can you say something about this?

Makungu Akinyela: At the heart of what we call a decolonial struggle, a decolonising struggle, is the idea of reclaiming dignity. Yes, it's political. It's about reclaiming health, reclaiming education, reclaiming housing. All those aspects that relate to human rights are important. But ultimately, it's about reclaiming dignity and reclaiming our own humanity.

For decades now, an important act within our people's struggle, particularly within the section of the struggle that I grew up in, is the act of naming ourselves, or what we call Kujichagulia: self-determination. The act of Kujichagulia, self-determination, involves naming ourselves, speaking for ourselves, creating for ourselves, and never letting anyone do it for us.

So for me, 50 years ago, as a young student activist, it was very important for me when someone chose a name for me that they believed fit my character, fit where I was in history, and that this was an African name. I then took this name to replace the European name that had been inherited from the slave owners of my ancestors, the name that had been imposed on them. When I did that, my mother was very hurt. She thought that I was dishonouring and disrespecting my grandfather. My father, on the other hand, understood that the same spirit of rebelliousness was actually a way of honouring my grandfather.

From my perspective, that name was not my grandfather's. It was the name that was imposed on him. I still honour and work in the spirit of my grandfather. But taking that African name for me was an important thing.

It was also very important for my wife, Chinganji, and I to be able to name our children, and they're very proud to say they have never had a slave name. They have never had names that reflected the European coloniser. The name that they carry is our family name—Akinyela. From our point of view, that act of Kujichagulia, that personal act of self-determination, makes it possible for us to even more fully participate in our collective cultural national self-determination as a people.

Can you tell me more about the history of this practice. Does it go a long way back?

We can look back at the early 20th century, in the Moorish Science Temple, founded by Noble Drew Ali, when brothers and sisters would take on what they called Moorish names. This is a question of identity, of resisting being identified by how our oppressors identify us. In the 1920s, the Moors would give themselves the name "Bay" or "El". They said, "That's my Moorish name. I'm a Moore. I'm not a negro, I'm a Moore". Around the same time, the Honourable Elijah Muhammad became the leader of the Nation of Islam, and when people joined that movement, they would take on the letter X to symbolise that they didn't know what their true name was, but they refused to carry the slave name, the name of the slave master. So, instead they carried the X. When Malcolm Little joined the Nation of Islam, he wrote a letter to the Honourable Elijah Muhammad and received his X, and from then on, he was known as Malcolm X.

Then later, he received his holy name, and he became Malik el-Shabazz. And because he went on Hajj, he's known as el-Hajj Malik el-Shabazz. When he went to West Africa, to Ghana, he was given a West African name. And so, he's also known to us as Omowale, which means "child returns home".

All of these were acts of naming, acts of self-determination, to move us away from our colonised slave identity towards our liberated African identities. They are a part of the overall movement for self-determination for African people.

Are there ways in which your name and this political tradition shapes your counselling conversations?

The principle of Kujichagulia, self-determination—that our people have a right to determine their own destinies—underlies all the work I do!

When it comes to the question of my name, I think the reality is my name becomes a signification to people in the marketplace. People find me, they come to me, because they see that name. Many people who were born in Africa see my African name and call me just for that reason. They want to know, "Are you African?" And I'll say, "Yes, I'm an African born in America". And people who carry European names, they see "Makungu Akinyela" and [snaps fingers] "That's a Black man", right? My name becomes a signifying marker that draws people who want to speak to an African.

We will often also have conversations about my name. People will ask, "Wait, well where did you get that name? How do you say that name? And what does it mean?" So then we'll talk about the meanings of my name and its political history. And I always work in transparency—I'll tell the story. And people resonate with the story. Even if it's not their own story of name changing, we begin our conversations in the context of talking about self-determination for African people. That sets a particular atmosphere for our collaborations.

They have often sought me out in the hope that I will understand the cultural contexts of their lives, that I will understand something of African cultures. My name becomes a signifying marker that helps people find some comfort and companionship.

Culture is complex, isn't it? And there are many African cultures. I really appreciate your writings in relation to critical Africentricity—how you understand cultures as living, changing realms; how you're not trying to "go back to something" but trying to continually create new cultural possibilities, drawing on and from traditions. I would be interested in how this political and critical framework influences your counselling conversations.

Let me respond in relation to my work with Black people. I mostly work with Black people, even though on occasion I have folks from other cultures in the room with me. When I'm working with Black people, the first way in which a critical Africana theory lens influences me is that I'm always aware that these folks in the room I'm talking with are Africans.

Not because they've necessarily got "African names". Not because they are maybe wearing "African clothes". They're Africans because they are the descendants of enslaved people who are now living a 21st century cultural life. They're bringing to me the problems of 21st century Africans living in this continent and carrying the histories of our people.

So I'm listening to the stories they're telling me, I'm listening to the problems they are bringing me, and I'm thinking about how these relate to the problems of 21st century Africans.

Let me give an example. I work mostly with heterosexual couples who are having conflicts. I'm very much aware of how gendered relationships between Black men and Black women have been shaped been our histories. We don't necessarily have that conversation, but I'm aware of it. So, if a heterosexual couple comes in and one partner is earning a much greater income than the other, and if they are having conflict related to finances, I'm thinking about a particular historical context.

Right after the Civil War, after the abolition of slavery, plantation owners had to start paying a salary to their former slaves. They may pay men 25 cents a day. If they hired women, they would pay them 5 cents a day. A year ago, they were all doing the same work that they are doing now. A year ago, they were all being paid the same price—nothing—because they were enslaved. But suddenly, because you're a man, you get 25 cents per day. Because you're a woman, you only get 5 cents. And oftentimes, women wouldn't be hired unless the employer could get the husband's permission for the woman to work.

These imposed policies created a whole mess of contradictions in gender relationships between Black men and women, which did not exist before. They set a whole pattern. Patterns of movement from rural areas to urban areas also changed things. In the urban areas, women could get jobs as maids, as cleaners, as cooks and the men couldn't get jobs. So now, a different economic power difference was created. Women in the cities were earning more and the men were less financially empowered. Policies shaping the lives of Black folks for centuries have had all sorts of effects on gender relationships, even up to this day.

So as I meet with heterosexual couples, I ask myself questions. "What are some of the assumptions that they're bringing in?" and "What might be the histories of these assumptions?" Not only about gender roles but also racialised assumptions: "This is what Black men do" or "as a Black woman …". I'm listening for any racialised assumptions in our conversation. And I'm thinking, and sometimes asking, "Where do these assumptions about gender relationships come from?"

I'm listening for all of that and I'm thinking about it in political ways, because I understand the history of racialised gendered relationships based on policies and rules and regulations that have shaped our people over time. I don't necessarily introduce a highly politicised conversation into the room, but I'll raise questions to invite the people who I'm working with to reflect on why they think what they think, why they're doing what they're doing. I may even raise cultural historical questions.

As someone influenced by critical Africana theory, I'm always thinking about the historical, social, cultural context of Black people. How is our political history and present shaping meanings in this individual or family situation, and how can I raise questions about this in the conversation.

That's really interesting to me. So where there are contemporary knots or complexity or problems in relationships, you are placing these within a broader social, cultural, political, historical context. Sometimes this is openly discussed, other times it informs your questions and approach. So in some ways this relates to a deconstruction of the problem informed by critical Africana studies. I'm also interested in how your critical Africana studies approach supports preferred storylines in your counselling work. The other day, as we were driving around Martinique, you spoke of how you are on the look out for moments when people might be acting or speaking in ways that could have resonances with preferred cultural traditions, whether or not these links have been explicitly made. Can you say more about this? How you might approach this, without reifying "traditional" culture?

As we're listening to these stories, these narratives, these testimonies, we're listening for what Michael White (2007) would have called "sparkling moments", those exceptions and stories that contradict the thin telling. I'm listening for victorious moments. Those parts of the testimony, the parts of the story, that show the person or family overcoming or being victorious in their life in contradiction to the doom and gloom story they've been telling. I'll listen for those moments and then the questions become:

– "Where did you learn that?"

– "Is there someone who taught you how to be like that in a situation?"

– "Can you remember any stories of elders or anybody else in your family who has done anything like that?"

And I might get to hear responses such as:

– "Well, yeah, my daddy was a drunk, but he used to still tell me bedtime stories, right? And those stories are really important to me."

Or,

- "He knew he couldn't do much, but, you know, his brother, would come and get me and take me places."

Or,

- "I had a coach in high school and she always used to encourage me."

And we start reflecting back to these other relationships. What we're trying to do is make reconnections to their kin network and to their histories. These are histories that relate to the victorious moments that emerge in their testimonies. I want to hear what else happened that moved them in that direction or that made possible that small victorious moment.

In this work, relationships become really important. We don't do anything on our own in isolation. We don't pull ourselves up by our own bootstraps. There's no magical miracle that enables people to do things on their own. It's always in relationship in some way. Even if it's in relationship to memories that include relational connections. So it's up to me to look for the relational connections and help people make those connections for themselves.

And once we start talking about these histories, these relationships, then we can speculate about the longer-term histories: how their grandparents faced the challenges of their day. And we can consider if there were certain principles or practices of culture that can be carried into today.

That sounds like a process of linking people to their own histories to enable further self-determination, Kujichagulia. Is that right?

Yes, every element of my work relates back to Kujichagulia.

Reference

White, M. (2007). *Maps of narrative practice.* Norton

9.
Rethinking Afrocentricity: The foundation of a theory of critical Africentricity

Over 90 years ago, WEB Du Bois (1989) wrote prophetically that the "problem of the 20th century" would be the problem of the colour line. The question of colour, race, ethnicity and tribe, while appearing to be subsumed after the Bolshevik revolution under the class struggle, has, as Du Bois so clearly envisioned, emerged in recent years as the premier defining and motivating force of the century.

That struggle has taken many forms. Whether it was Du Bois's own Niagara Movement, Garvey's UNIA, Cesaire's Negritude, Nkrumah's Pan-Africanism, the religious nationalism of the Nation of Islam, the Soul Force of the civil rights movement, the cultural and revolutionary Black nationalism of the 1960s, or Steve Biko's Black Consciousness in South Africa, the "problem of the 20th century" has remained at the centre of historical development and change in the world. All of these trends attest to the long history in the African diaspora of African-centred, hence Afrocentric, social, political and cultural discourse. They have been the development of the Afrocentric idea (Asante, 1987) as a theoretical construct in itself.

In malls and storefronts across the United States, shops specialising in Afrocentric clothing, books, art and other commodities are flourishing. The "X" worn on caps, shirts and buttons by millions of US-born Africans has in many ways taken on a life of its own beyond identification with Malcolm X and has come to symbolise simply the wearer's attempts to establish links with an Afrocentric identity. New Afrikan teachers and administrators have come together for several "immersion conferences" to discuss and share ideas on practical implementation of Afrocentric content throughout the curriculum in public and private schools (Hilliard et al., 1990). Some of the fastest-growing churches in large urban centres are those that are part of the so-called neo-Pentecostal movement (Lincoln & Mumiya, 1990) that focuses on both an Afrocentric cultural and political perspective and a charismatic worship style. Practical research and theoretical construction are being implemented in the fields of psychology (Akbar, 1985; Nobles, 1985), history (Carruthers, 1984; Keto, 1989), ethics (Karenga, 1984), political theory (Karenga, 1980; T'Shaka, 1990), and other disciplines. Afrocentricity is a significant and growing movement within the New Afrikan communities and among both African and European American intellectuals and academics. As the Afrocentricity movement has grown, there has been a corresponding growth of theoretical and philosophical literature that defines, describes and shapes the direction of the movement. This chapter will examine the social and political implications of Afrocentric theoretical models put forth by several leading Afrocentric thinkers as these models are applied to existing cultural situations. Particular focus will be applied to the Afrocentric intellectual ideas of Molefi K Asante, Maulana Karenga and others. I will also begin the task of offering a critique of the dominant Afrocentric intellectual trend. Finally, I will suggest a rethinking of the Afrocentric paradigm that will lay the foundation for a theory of critical Africentricity.[1]

Defining Afrocentricity

Afrocentricity refers to an intellectual discourse that is concerned with integrating an interdisciplinary field of study from a common world view. Afrocentricity is the philosophical basis for Black studies (Karenga, 1982) or, as some call it, Afrology—the study of Africa, Africans and related issues (Asante, 1987). Asante (1983) stated that Afrocentricity is "the logical heir to Negritude". In *The Afrocentric Idea in Education* (1991), he wrote:

> Afrocentricity is a frame of reference wherein phenomena are viewed from the perspective of the African person. The Afrocentric approach seeks in every situation the appropriate centrality of the African person. (Asante, 1991, p. 5)

Defining a *classical paradigm* is essential to Afrocentric thought and praxis. Bayo Oyebade (1990) wrote:

> Since Afrocentricity adopts Africa as a takeoff point in any discussion of African civilization, it is Diopian in methodology. Indeed the Diopian school of Afrocentric thought insists that the ancient Kemetic (Egyptian) civilization should be the classical reference point for the study of African civilization, as the Greek civilization is for analysis of European civilization. (Oyebade, 1990, p. 234)

Karenga (1988), who is the creator of his own Afrocentric sociopolitical theory, which he calls Kawaida, also relying on Diop, wrote:

> [The Afrocentric] world view must evolve from the rescue and reconstruction of the classical African legacy of Egypt. Diop … writes that "for us, the return to Egypt in all fields is the necessary condition to build a body of modern human sciences, and renew African culture." In fact, "Egypt will play, in a rethought and

renewed African culture, the same role that the ancient Greco-Latin civilizations play in Western culture." (Karenga, 1988, p. 411, quoting from Diop, 1981)

Both Oyabade and Karenga see the use of ancient Egyptian civilisation's classical paradigm as a fundamental step towards establishing the groundwork of modern Black civilisation. The question of an authentic African-centred way of knowing the world and an African epistemology, as well as an African-centred ontology, is essential to Oyabade, Asante, Karenga and other Afrocentric writers. Norman Harris (1992) wrote that:

> The significance of Afrocentric ontology and epistemology is profound. The way one constructs reality, one's place in it, and the way one validates knowledge determines one's life chances. For example, the individualistic ontology into which we have all been socialized makes it all but impossible for many African Americans to conceptualize the idea of racial responsibility, particularly as it relates to racial empowerment. (Harris, 1992, p. 156)

Harris asserted that the questions of individualism and communalism are key differentiations between Eurocentric and Afrocentric ontologies. This communal Afrocentric ontology stretches beyond human relationships into the African relationship with nature, which humans, from an Afrocentric perspective, should be in harmony with. Harris located Afrocentric epistemology in a combination of historical knowledge and personal intuition. He continued,

> History is key because when the individual appropriately submerges himself in the reservoir of African history, then that submersion allows the individual to discover him or herself in the context of that history and thereby judge the reality of any given phenomenon. (Harris, 1992, p. 157)

The concept of a centrist worldview and cultural perspective that makes the observers subjects in their own discourse is the starting point of Afrocentric theory. This counter-hegemonic strike against Euro-American domination of cultural discourse in a multicultural society is of great importance. However, there are some problematic areas within the discourse of Afrocentricity that must be examined in order to move it to a truly counter-hegemonic position.

The problems of Afrocentricity

The basic Afrocentric argument of a need to create a major shift in the hegemonic Eurocentric epistemology, which also sets the foundation of US society, is a correct one. However, Afrocentrists generally tend to reduce the issue of Eurocentric epistemological hegemony to an issue of racial proclivity (biological determinism) and ethnic domination. A deeper economic and political analysis of hegemonic Eurocentric culture and structuring of society will provide a more functional understanding of the sociopolitical and cultural solutions to the New Afrikan situation in the United States.

It could be argued effectively that there is no monolithic European culture, though there is a European cultural ethos dominated by one class view. Eurocentric culture as we know it today is largely a product of the coming to power of the bourgeois merchant class in Europe, and later in the Americas, over the European aristocracy within the past 500 years. The culture of the European bourgeoisie with all of its accompanying philosophical assumptions has guided the thinking of most Europeans and affected the lives of New Afrikans[2] and other colonised and formerly colonised peoples in the world.

Asante's argument cited above and his focus on making African people subjects of their own lived experience, rather than objects of European and Euro-American study, is relevant and necessary. This also raises the question of the place and possibility of intellectual objectivity in the study of human societies and sociopolitical relationships. The myth of intellectual objectivity has historically been used as a tool of repression by the European and Euro-American bourgeoisie to maintain a position of power in matters of race, gender, culture and social discourse. This has allowed the mainly white male bourgeoisie to set the parameters of academic legitimacy and limit the control of intellectual discourse to white men of that class or those people of colour and white women culturally loyal to that class.

The ideology of the Eurocentric bourgeoisie was born out of the matrix of the Protestant Reformation, the development of capitalism and the expansion of European imperialism in the 15th century. The ideological development of the European bourgeoisie occurred in the historical context of ongoing contention between the mercantile capitalist class and the last remnants of the Roman Empire represented by the European aristocracy and the Roman Catholic Church.

The new bourgeois class striving to break the restrictive, anti-intellectual bonds of the Roman Catholic Church sought a model for the new society that the class was striving to shape. The new bourgeois society that they envisioned, unlike the powerful Church of Rome, was open to new knowledge and learning. The leaders of the European Enlightenment found a model for the new society in the precursor to Rome—Ancient Greece.

By the 18th and 19th centuries, the new class ideology was firmly entrenched as the ruling paradigm. The age of reason and "science", guided by the classic Greco-Roman ethos and aesthetic, had propelled Europe and the European-dominated Americas into the position of political, economic and intellectual rulers of the world. All of the leading influential thinkers of Europe would base their ideas on the Greek paradigm. Freud would use names from Greek mythology (id, ego, super-ego, Oedipal complex) to describe his theory of human psychoanalysis. Max Weber (1958) would write in *The Protestant Ethic and the Spirit of Capitalism*:

> Only in the West does science exist at a stage of development which we recognize today as valid. Empirical knowledge, reflection on problems of the cosmos and of life, philosophical and theological wisdom of the most profound sort, are not

confined to it, though in the case of the last the full development of a systematic theology must be credited to Christianity under the influence of Hellenism In short, knowledge and observation of great refinement have existed elsewhere, above all in India, China, Babylonia, and Egypt. But in Babylonia and elsewhere astronomy lacked—which makes its development all the more astounding—the mathematical foundation which it first received from the Greeks. (Weber, 1958, p. 13)

The obvious Eurocentrism of Weber, writing in the 19th century, is placed in context by the work of Cornel West (1982), who is very helpful in explaining the relationship between the establishment of the Greek paradigm and the historical development of the European bourgeois class during the European Enlightenment.

> The Enlightenment revolt against the authority of the church and the search for models of unrestrained criticism led to a highly charged recovery of classical antiquity, and especially to a new appreciation and appropriation of the artistic and cultural heritage of ancient Greece. For our purposes, the classical revival is important because it infuses Greek ocular metaphors and classical ideals of beauty, proportion, and moderation into the beginnings of modern discourse. Greek ocular metaphors—eye of the mind, mind as mirror of nature, mind as inner arena with its inner observer—dominate modern discourse in the West. … Modern philosophical inquiry is saddled with the epistemological model of intellect (formerly Plato's and Aristotle's Nous, now Descartes's Inner Eye) inspecting entities modeled on retinal images, with the Eye of the Mind viewing representations in order to find some characteristic that would testify to their fidelity. The creative fusion of scientific investigation, Cartesian philosophy, Greek ocular metaphors, and classical aesthetic and cultural ideals constitutes the essential elements of modern discourse in the West. (West, 1982, p. 53)

Therefore, we can see how Eurocentric bourgeois ideology, focused on notions of class, racial, gender and sexual hierarchy and domination, can in the name of reason, science and the Greek paradigm come to be the basis for maintaining the "status quo". Moreover, this ideology of reason, science and materialism relies on a dichotomous world view that splits object from subject, mental from physical and masculine from feminine, and attempts to reduce the world to essentials, ultimate truths, classical forms and good or bad representations. In the end, this represents a static, noncritical world view, even when it has been presented in the form of the historical materialism of Marxist philosophy.

The limitations of Afrocentricity

This bourgeois dichotomisation of reality is precisely the place where the limitations within Afrocentricity emerge. If Afrocentricity is uncritical in its approach, it may only succeed in taking bourgeois Eurocentric thought, turning it on its philosophical head, painting it black and calling it African. Asante (1991) specifically denied that this is the case. He wrote:

> It must be emphasized that Afrocentricity is not a Black version of Eurocentricity. Eurocentricity is based on white supremacist notions whose purposes are to protect white privilege and advantage in education, economics, politics, and so forth. Unlike Eurocentricity, Afrocentricity does not condone ethnocentric valorization at the expense of degrading other groups' perspectives. (Asante, 1991, p. 171)

However, by focusing primarily on that aspect of bourgeois Eurocentric thought that emphasises racial supremacy, while not fully assessing the dichotomous and essentialist nature of bourgeois thought as problematic in itself, Asante is able to avoid a critique of the dichotomous and essentialist nature of his own theories. This Afrocentricity implicitly accepts bourgeois theories of knowledge and cultural construction even while arguing for a new epistemological and ontological paradigm. This implicit acceptance of bourgeois philosophy often results in what appears to be empty worship and glorification of ancient "classical" knowledge and Kemetic esoterica while ignoring the ongoing construction of knowledge in the reflection of current African peoples on their lived experiences. The fact remains that failure to see the class basis and connection of Afrocentricity to bourgeois Eurocentric thought in fact often does lead to Asante's description of "ethnocentric valorization at the expense of degrading other groups' perspectives".

The question of the nature of knowledge is most significant to this discussion. Knowledge does not rest in an eternal pool somewhere waiting for an aware human being to come and appropriate it and "pass it along". This traditional notion is the "banking" concept of knowledge challenged by Paulo Freire (1990). Yet Afrocentrists often conceive of knowledge in this way when they speak of "going back to the ancient Kemetic knowledge". The banking approach to knowledge, which emphasises a teacher-to-student hierarchy, serves to keep ownership of knowledge and culture from those who are coparticipants in constructing it. The effort to set up a classical baseline of knowledge as "source" and canon becomes a political issue in that the implicit seat of power rests with those who define and are most familiar with the canon and its parameters. Bell hooks (1990) wrote that this dualism ultimately lends legitimacy to existing Eurocentric ideas:

> It is no mere accident of fate that the ground of current discourse on black subjectivity is cultural terrain. Art remains that site of imaginative possibility where "anything goes," particularly if one is not seeking to create a hot commodity for the marketplace. Black folks' inability to envision liberatory paradigms of black subjectivity in a purely political realm is in part a failure of critical imagination. Yet even on cultural ground discussions of black subjectivity are often limited to the topic of representation, good and bad images, or contained by projects concerned with

reclaiming and/or inventing traditions (expressed in literary circles by the issue of canon formation). Interestingly, both these endeavors are not in any essential way oppositional. Focus on good and bad images may be more fundamentally connected to the western metaphysical dualism that is the philosophical underpinning of racist and sexist domination than with radical efforts to reconceptualize black cultural identities. Concurrently, focus on canon formation legitimates the creative work of black writers in academic circles while reinforcing white hegemonic authorial canonicity. (hooks, 1990, p. 18)

The question must be asked whether Afrocentrists, by focusing on the so-called baseline knowledge of "classical" African civilisations, are in fact lending credence to the use of Greek civilisation as the baseline of bourgeois Eurocentric cultural hegemony. This would imply that Afrocentrists do not see the accumulation of political power, control of knowledge and cultural hegemony by one class in society over other classes as problematic in itself.

Consequently, Afrocentrists do tend to assume an avoidance posture towards questions of conflict, power and politics. This ties Afrocentricity strongly to the Black cultural nationalism of the 1960s, which emphasised a dualistic separation of "political" struggle and "cultural" struggle, assuming that the cultural struggle must be won prior to and distinct from the political struggle. This cultural nationalism was marked also by a denial of the political significance of class contradictions and power inequalities among New Afrikans. For example, Karenga, as chair of the cultural nationalist "Us Organization", could say in 1967,

We say with [Sékou] Touré that for Us there are no intellectuals, no students, no workers, no teachers; there are only supporters of the organization ... We do not accept the idea of class struggle; for today in Afro-America there is but one class, an oppressed class [of Blacks]. (Karenga, 1967, p. 25)

Today, Afrocentricity as a theoretical model has failed to develop a class analysis that takes into account the significance of political and economic power differences and the problems that may arise within the African community as a result. Asante (1990) provided a descriptive assessment of class relationships, which seems to be based on Weberian notions of class structure, but which again does not extend sufficiently to assess the political significance of this structure:

> Class distinctions for the Afrocentrist consist in four aspects of property relations: (1) those who possess income producing properties, (2) those who possess some property that produces income and a job that supplements income, (3) those who maintain professions or positions because of skills, and (4) those who do not have skills and whose services may or may not be employed. (Asante, 1990, p. 10)

Asante (1988) went no further in his analysis of class structure because within his theoretical framework, analysis focused on class contradictions is based on a Eurocentric model of conflict. This idea of historical conflict being Eurocentric and antithetical to Afrocentrism is reflected in Asante's critique of Marxism:

> Marxism ... allows open warfare on the bourgeois class. Operating on the European values of confrontation developed from the adventures of Europeans during the terrible White Ages, both of these systems (capitalism and Marxism) believe in utter destruction of aliens. This, of course, is contradictory to the Afrocentric value which respects difference and applauds pluralism. Strangers exist in that they have not been known ... [but] Marxism's Eurocentric foundation makes it antagonistic to our worldview; its confrontational nature does not provide the spiritual satisfaction we have found in our history of harmony. (Asante, 1988, p. 79)

The Afrocentricity of Asante and other leading thinkers stresses an avoidance of conflict with the capitalist system and poses solutions that remain in the context of existing capitalism. Asante (1988) asserted:

> We must struggle to gain a foothold in every sector of the American economy. Our path to economic survival will not be based upon landholdings but owning secure industries, creative breakthroughs in art and music, exploitation of all fields of athletics and salaried positions based on education and talent. (Asante, 1988, p. 94)

This failure to confront asymmetrical power relations outside of a cultural critique of Eurocentric racism within existing capitalist society is a serious weakness of Afrocentricity. By secluding the Afrocentric view to primarily a critique of white racist ideology, the Afrocentrists seem to be carving out a comfortable and acceptable Afrocentric niche for themselves in established Eurocentric academia. The primary emphasis of this academic Afrocentrism seems to be in promoting a pluralistic, multicultural society where no one culture has hegemony over any other, yet it resists the idea of conflict or antagonism, which would seem to be necessary in overcoming the power inequities inherent in current political cultural relations. These political cultural relations are evident in disproportionate poverty, disease, crime, police oppression and other realities of the lived experience of New Afrikans in US cities.

The dichotomous, static and ahistorical view of knowledge prevalent in Afrocentric discourse reflects the hegemonic influence of bourgeois Eurocentric thought on Afrocentric writers even as they strive to construct "pure" Afrocentric epistemologies. The reification of culture and the focus on ancient civilisations (and more specifically, the ruling classes of those civilisations as models for current Afrocentric social structure) betrays an apparent desire to replicate European hierarchical social structure, even as Afrocentrists criticise Eurocentric society. Asante (1988, p. 47) wrote, "Walking the way of the new world means that we must establish schools which will teach our children how to behave like the kings and queens they are meant to be". Little or no mention is made in Afrocentric writing of the role of the ancient African peasantry and the labourers who actually constructed the ancient monuments of Kemet, Ethiopia and Great Zimbabwe. The illusion is maintained that these human efforts were all accomplished in totally harmonious relations, with each person, whether king or labourer, male or female, mystically happy to stay in their place assigned by the universe.

This harmonious social order is the key to civilisation for the Afrocentrists, who insist that there were no antagonisms or class contradictions in the "classical" civilisations. However, this view is not even upheld by the patriarch of many Afrocentrists, Cheikh Anta Diop. Diop (1974) described a revolutionary situation that occurred in the 6th Dynasty of the Old Kingdom of Kemet under the Pharaoh Zoser, who clashed with the priests of the city of Heliopolis and proclaimed himself "Great God" and outside of the control of any human authority. Diop wrote:

> Thereafter the regime again evolved toward feudalism. The courtiers constituted a special corps of dignitaries which would make itself hereditary by usage and soon by right. The feudal system that had just triumphed with the Fifth Dynasty reached its peak with the Sixth. It then engendered general stagnation in the economy and the administration of the State in urban as well as rural areas. And the Sixth Dynasty was to end with the first popular uprising in Egyptian history. (Diop, 1974, p. 206)

The target of the uprising was the oppressive state bureaucracy, which most affected the Egyptian poor. The rebellion challenged the absolute political and religious power of the pharaoh, which even reached to the grave. According to the theology of the time, only the pharaoh had a right to the "Osirian death" or the hope of resurrection. "After that revolution," wrote Diop, "all Egyptians had a right to the 'Osirian death.' … The discontent was strong enough completely to disrupt Egyptian society throughout the entire country" (1974, p. 207).

It is evident in Diop's research that the "classical" Kemetic civilisation was (1) repressive and divided by class contradiction, and (2) historically changed and democratised by antagonism and conflict between the classes, in spite of the Afrocentrist assertion that conflict is antithetical to the African ideal of social harmony.

When considered in this light, Afrocentricity (like bourgeois Eurocentricity) seems more concerned with codifying knowledge, history and social structure into a status quo that can only be comprehended and defined by a chosen few. Repeated references to harmony as a principle, while ignoring the existence of unequal social relations of power, functions to maintain power in the hands of those who define the arena of discourse.

Asante is correct when he says that Afrocentricity is the legitimate heir of Negritude. But like the philosophical movement of the Franco-African petty bourgeoisie, Afrocentricity is vulnerable to the same critique that was so eloquently levelled by Frantz Fanon (1963). Speaking of the colonised African intellectual struggling to find a place for himself in his own society, Fanon wrote:

> Thus we see that the cultural problem as it sometimes exists in colonized countries runs the risk of giving rise to serious ambiguities ... Culture is becoming more and more cut off from the events of today ... It is true that the attitude of the native intellectual sometimes takes on the aspect of a cult or of a religion ... He sets a high value on the customs, traditions, and the appearances of his people; but his inevitable, painful experience only seems to be a banal search for exoticism. (Fanon, 1963, p. 217, 221)

Fanon pointed out that this effort to codify traditions and place virtual religious value on reconstructing the past out of forgotten cultural practices is in conflict with the nature of cultural knowledge. Asante with his Njia system (1988) and Karenga with Kawaida thought (1967) have focused on constructing whole new cultural, religious systems that are based on "classical" African ethos, customs and traditions. These systems codify the past, and it is emphasised that their acceptance and practice are minimal requirements for "authentic" Afrocentric cultural praxis. There is an underlying suggestion in these systems that the lived historical culture of New Afrikans is somehow less than African because it lacks "purity" due to contamination by Euro-American culture. Culture is not a static set of customs, formulas or traditions. To attempt to locate culture in specific customs, traditions and ways of thinking that are not allowed to change actually leads to the death of culture. I agree with Fanon (1963) that "the desire to attach oneself to tradition or bring abandoned traditions to life again does not only mean going against the current of history but also opposing one's own people" (p. 224).

Fanon warned that *this* static search for a reconstruction of the "glorious past" and defining what is "African" according to the petty bourgeois intellectuals is problematic in that this class often ends up simply replacing white masters with Black ones. At the same time, no fundamental changes in the structure of society are made. The legitimacy of the status quo is maintained in the name of reconstructing and preserving so-called pure African culture. It is probably no coincidence that Afrocentrists and cultural nationalists in the United States have often been the most vocal supporters of dictators like Mobutu in Zaire, Amin in Uganda, Burnham in Guyana, the Duvaliers in Haiti, and many other despots who have exploited and oppressed Africans for their own ends. All of these men have done so while supposedly promoting "traditional" African customs and culture.

Rethinking Afrocentricity

Do these criticisms mean that Afrocentricity as an intellectual discipline and theoretical model should be abandoned? On the contrary, while some New Afrikan intellectuals have condemned Afrocentricity as irrelevant or reactionary (Gates, 1991; Steele, 1990), Afrocentricism's strongest argument is in its call for a counter-hegemonic discourse to break the intellectual and moral legitimacy of the Eurocentric bourgeoisie on the minds and lives of the African, Asian and Latin American world majority. I would add that it is strategically necessary to total human liberation to also break the hegemonic domination on the minds and lives of working people of European descent who are also in cultural and political control of the ruling classes.

The Afrocentric claim—that African people must construct a new African identity and must begin to perceive and interpret the world in its entirety from an African psychological, spiritual and cultural frame of reference—is a correct one. Africans must engage with problems and issues from our own contexts as subjects in the world. This is not a neutral project. It requires an ongoing critical assessment of both subjective lived experience and objective conditions.

The major weakness of Afrocentricity exists in limiting its social critique to the role of white supremacist racism and abstracting and dehistoricising culture in its relationship to politics and power. Afrocentricity for the most part implicitly accepts the legitimacy of static, positivist epistemology. In its refusal to deepen the critique of existing capitalist social structure and capitalism's relationship to oppression and exploitation, Afrocentricity implicitly accepts the legitimacy of the politics of domination outside of the racial paradigm and fails to examine the relationship to racism of other forms of oppression such as sexism, heterosexism and ecological destruction at this point in history.

I would argue that some form of Afrocentric theory is necessary in this historical period in which, while there are no significant legal restrictions to Black freedom, New Afrikans of all classes are expressing more cynicism and despair about the relationship between Africans and US social and political life. It is also a time when the New Afrikan urban poor, employed and unemployed, are feeling isolated and powerless in a society where the majority of Euro-Americans and even some middle-class people of colour are demanding more tax cuts, less spending, more jails, more police and less government help for affirmative action programs.

This social, political and cultural context seems to call for a radical world view with a vision of a restructured society. The restructured society developed out of the new world view would be one committed to cultural democracy and equality for the various ethnic, sexual, class and other groups within the society. This new world view would be culturally centrist and committed to critical analysis of both the state and civil societies.

A theory of critical Africentricity

Critical Africentricity is a philosophy of praxis aimed at creating effective strategies of liberation from the multiple forms of domination experienced by African people born in the United States in particular, and African people throughout the diaspora in general. Because critical Africentric theory is related to critical pedagogy and is concerned with developing a humanitarian world view, it is also aimed at developing and participating in a worldwide liberatory practice that will benefit all of humanity. For the critical Africentrist, the discourse of social analysis about Africans in America is derived from both an understanding of the precolonial African experience and the collective lived experiences of New Afrikans in the struggle against racial colonialism.

In rethinking some of the issues of Afrocentricity, and applying a critical Africentric analysis, I will look at four major questions: (1) the nature of culture; (2) the construction of knowledge; (3) hegemony, power and political oppression; and (4) critical Africentricity and consciousness. In the following section I will further explain the key issues that define critical Africentric theory.

Critical Africentricity and the nature of culture

Definitions of culture are usually either anthropological, focusing on what particular cultures look like, or they are sociological, focusing on lists of elements of culture. Most definitions of culture assume that culture is an expression of monolithic ethnic/racial communities through phenomena such as art, food, music, clothing, religion or other outward forms. In the same vein, Karenga (1980) listed seven elements in his Afrocentric Kawaida theory, which he said that every culture possesses.[3]

Critical Africentric understanding of culture would posit that cultural phenomena take their form in the dialectical tension that exists in the asymmetrical power relationships between groups and within groups. Culture is constructed as the more powerful and the less powerful segments of society contend for positions of power and privilege. This means that any given culture is actually a complex of cultures between unequal class, gender, religious, language, sexual and other elements within groups. HE Newsum (1990) described how this phenomenon functions between language groups:

> Intergroup activities between members of opposed sociolinguistic and socioeconomic realities produce a language which reflects the class roles of persons acting in the situation and sometimes there is noticeable condescension on the part of the upper class participants and defiance or passiveness on the part of lower class participants. ... The consciousness of exploiting groups and the consciousness of exploited groups respectively are in constant opposition, each group advancing the collective cause of the two respective divisions. (Newsum, 1990, p. 23)

As Newsum explained from his perspective as a sociolinguist, these systems of culture are defined by often oppositional individual and collective subject positions within a society. This is the dialectic of culture. This notion suggests that there are really no homogeneous national cultures so much as systems of contending social groups within national groups or ethnicities, which are in constant struggle with one another over positions of power and influence.

A cultural dialectic occurs between economic classes, geographical locations, colour/caste groups, religious sects and denominations, language dialect groups, sexual orientation groups, gender groups, and perhaps other currently unrecognisable groupings, all within the context of New Afrikan ethnicity. This same cultural dialectic that occurs within ethnocultural groups also exists between such groups. For instance, as the New Afrikan middle class strives to place its values at the centre of the agenda to define Black people's social and political direction, there is a response from the New Afrikan poor and working class, both in defence of their own values and in an effort to exert itself and survive as a group. Yet, even in the contention, there is mutual influence between groups.

This, then, is an argument against notions of cultural purity and permanence. It is the nature of culture to adopt from and adapt to outside influences, both as acts of resistance and as acts of domination striving for recognition from the other. Culture is constructed in the constant process of dynamic change motivated by shifts in asymmetrical power relationships within complexes of various subject positions. The resulting material manifestations of cultural phenomena—for example the artistic, social and political expressions of groups and individuals—are acts of resistance and survival, which assist and motivate cultural actors to make sense of and give meaning to their collective existence. At best, we can only identify cultural historical moments in any civilisation's process, as opposed to identifying classical paradigms that define a culture for all time.

From this perspective, rather than accepting the notion that Black people in the United States have been passive objects of a process of de-Africanisation and Americanisation, they can be understood as being active subjects in the process of Africanising the European culture that they encountered. Whatever religious, linguistic, familial or sociopolitical form was thrust upon them has been appropriated, internalised and Africanised into the collective ethos. There is no need to seek "pure" classical African cultural forms to prove the Africanity of Blacks in the United States. There have never been such forms, even on the continent.

Critical Africentricity and knowledge

Critical Africentricity maintains a historical view of knowledge. Knowledge is socially constructed and culturally mediated within societies and is affected by historical context. Human beings construct knowledge in their critical reflection on lived experiences, out of which they are able to define and name their own sociopolitical reality.

Antonia Darder (1991) spoke to the importance of constructing knowledge from the lived histories of oppressed peoples:

> With this in mind, a critical approach must appropriate [oppressed people's] own histories by delving into their own biographies and systems of meaning ... A critical perspective opposes the positivist emphasis on historical continuities and historical development. In its place is found a mode of analysis that stresses the breaks, discontinuities, and tensions in history, all which become valuable in that they highlight the centrality of human agency and struggle while simultaneously revealing the gap between society as it presently exists and society as it might be. (Darder, 1991, p. 80)

These "stresses and breaks" are the contradictions, situations and problems to be solved between individuals and social groups in order for society to prosper. These social group issues are the motive force of history and the locus of the construction of knowledge. This challenges both the notion of pure classical knowledge, which is handed down from one generation to the next, and the idea that societies can be perfected by reconstructing old systems and traditions of knowledge, as well as the notion of knowledge as an individual pursuit.

People act as subjects in the world on objects of knowledge. These objects of knowledge may be environmental material conditions, social historical situations, challenges of nature or psycho-spiritual challenges. Using information gained from "old knowledge", subjects reflect, share and strive to understand as a community. In the act of challenging new situations and problems, "new knowledge" is constructed, which will eventually itself become "old knowledge" to be challenged by new situations. This construction, challenge and new construction of knowledge provides the context in which, as Fanon (1963) said, "each generation must out of relative obscurity, discover its mission, fulfill it or betray it" (p. 206).

Hegemony, power and political oppression

Gramsci's (1949) concepts of domination and hegemony are helpful in a discussion of the relationship between power and political oppression. Prior to the civil rights movement, the primary means of colonial control of New Afrikans was by domination. The use of direct force, violence and intimidation through laws, police, the military and civilian forces was sufficient to keep the people of the colonised ghetto in place. In more recent years, since the fall of Jim Crow segregation, global capitalism in the United States has tended to rely primarily on cultural hegemony and only secondarily on domination as a means of social control.

While Afrocentrists have raised the issue of hegemony in discussions of culture, they have used the term mainly in its instrumental form, referring mostly to cultural or ideological predominance. Critical Africentricity understands hegemony as the psychological and social manipulation of one or several groups by another group for the purpose of establishing moral and intellectual leadership. Hegemony is the gained consent of a group to the domination by another group even when the consent may not be in the interest of the consenting group. Hegemony is enforced primarily through the institutions of civil society, which are the cultural institutions such as churches, social clubs, sororities/fraternities, educational institutions, artistic institutions, print and electronic media, and private enterprise. All of these institutions of "civil society" are to varying degrees independent from the state and its apparatus.

The core of US cultural hegemony is based on maintaining the myth of a common and collective heritage for "all Americans" regardless of race, creed or national origin. This myth is symbolised in various ways by Plymouth Rock, Thanksgiving, the American Revolution, the Liberty Bell, the Constitution and various other representations. Cultural hegemony is codified in the manufacturing of a common desire, the ubiquitous "American Dream". Hegemony and desire are manufactured in songs; hair spray, deodorant and automobile commercials; movies; novels and comic books. The theme of this hegemonic desire is always the same: "You ought to want this fantasy life. And if you work hard enough it can be yours."

Hegemony is exerted by what is allowed in the cultural discourse and what is discouraged or muted from the discourse. When ideas are discounted, denied or ignored, possibilities and alternatives are cut off. The targets of hegemony are forced to "settle" for what they are presented with and can only figure that "this is the best (country, car, economic system, solution to racism) there is". This is the manner in which false or uninformed consent is garnered, through legitimation and delegitimation. Hence the main objective of cultural hegemony is to create an assimilated society under the leadership of the ruling class to ensure the smooth running of the dominant system. When assimilation fails, domination and intimidation result.

Critical Africentricity and consciousness

Consciousness is closely related to the question of hegemony. Consciousness is the personal awareness possessed by individuals of shared collective experience and connected interests with a group in the context of common social, political and cultural conditions. Consciousness may be identified within and by the group according to specific discoveries related to racial, class, ethnic, national or other collective experience.

Consciousness is primarily a subjective act of collective will. It is constructed in the social engagement of humans with each other and the environment. Material conditions play a part in shaping consciousness; however, the subjective wills of collectives acting on their environment are primary.

Critical Africentricity posits the need to develop a collective liberatory consciousness as a necessary act against Eurocentric control of New Afrikans. Both Malcolm X (Perry, 1989) and Frantz Fanon (1963) focused on counter-hegemonic action as the source of liberatory consciousness. This is also the locus identified by critical Africentric theory. Again, there is agreement with Afrocentric and cultural nationalist thought in identifying the need to gain moral cultural authority in the hearts and minds of the oppressed through cultural revolution. Where critical Africentricity differs from cultural nationalism and Afrocentricity is at the crucial points of misidentifying the reconstruction of classical civilisation and cultural traditions as the primary ground of resistance and of identifying the so-called cultural revolution as a separate and prior act to political revolution. Critical Africentricity posits that these are mutually interrelated processes. Cultural action is political, and politics is cultural action. As discussed earlier, because these Afrocentric/cultural nationalist pursuits are based on the implicit acceptance of Eurocentric cultural assumptions, they in fact serve to reinforce the legitimacy of Eurocentric hegemony. Afrocentricity therefore ends up serving as part of oppressive, hegemonic civil society. In contrast, counter-hegemonic cultural action seeks to discredit or refute the pillars of the dominant value system, not legitimate them by posing similar, though "Afrocentric", values and assumptions about social structure, history and epistemology.

Conclusion

Critical Africentricity can be summed up by outlining nine major characteristics of its theory and praxis. These are the components that form the basis for the theory and that define critical Africentricity as a distinct theory from Afrocentricity.

1. Critical Africentricity is a cultural/social theory based on a dynamic epistemology drawn from the historical and current experiences of New Afrikans born in the United States.

2. Critical Africentricity is dedicated to self-determination as essential to the liberation of New Afrikans born in the United States.

3. Critical Africentricity refuses to accept cultural compartmentalising of knowledge based on false notions of biological determinism and racialism. For the critical Africentrist, all knowledge is potentially useful for freedom.

4. Critical Africentricity values African cultural knowledge and traditions and emphasises its historicity and ongoing change against notions of "classic", unchanging forms of cultural knowledge.

5. Critical Africentricity emphasises cultural historical identification with Africa by New Afrikans as essential both to ethnic/cultural survival and as a means of resistance to racial colonialism and cultural hegemony.

6. Critical Africentricity utilises a dialectical social analysis that opposes the stratification of society along unequal ethnic, class, gender and sexual lines.

7. Critical Africentricity posits that there are contradictions such as racialism, sexism, heterosexism and ecological domination that are transhistorical (not dependent on and prior to) capitalism. To challenge the legitimacy of these interrelated social contradictions is a necessary revolutionary act for social change.

8. Critical Africentricity is committed to radical democracy and a redistribution of economic, political, social and cultural assets and power.

9. Critical Africentricity posits that the development of a national cultural consciousness by New Afrikans as a people for themselves is a necessary counter-hegemonic strategic action towards liberation from racial colonialism, capitalism and cultural domination.

These criteria can serve as a guide in developing further work and praxis around critical Africentricity, emphasising the radical struggle against bourgeois philosophy, whether it is African or European. Critical Africentricity seeks to break down the dualistic divisions between cultural discourse and political discourse. It is a challenge for us to value the everyday experience of common people as the place to begin defining what is real. This everyday experience is the place from which New Afrikans will shape their own liberation. At its best, critical Africentricity should be cultural action for the freedom of a colonised people.

Notes

1. The form Africentricity is used rather than Afrocentricity to distinguish the two theories and to highlight that the term is a contraction of African-centric. Or in the words of Queen Mother Audley Moore, "Ain't no such land as Afro-land!"
2. Hereafter, I will refer to "New Afrikans" as a cultural/national identification for Africans born in the United States as distinguished from Continental and other diaspora African national groups.
3. Karenga's (1980) seven elements are: mythology; history; social organisation; economic organisation; political organisation; creative motif; ethos.

References

Akbar, N. (1985). *The community of self*. Mind.

Asante, M. K. (1983). The ideological significance of Afrocentricity in intercultural communication. *Journal of Black Studies, 14*(1), 3–19. https://doi.org/10.1177/002193478 301400

Asante, M. K. (1987). *The Afrocentric idea*. Temple University Press.

Asante, M. K. (1988). *Afrocentricity*. Africa World Press.

Asante, M. K. (1990). *Kemet, Afrocentricity and knowledge*. Africa World Press.

Asante, M. K. (1991). The Afrocentric idea in education. *Journal of Negro Education, 60*(2), 170–180. https://doi.org/10.2307/2295608

Carruthers, J. H. (1984). *Essays in ancient Egyptian studies*. University of Sankore Press.

Darder, A. (1991). *Culture and power in the classroom: A critical foundation for bicultural education*. Bergin and Garvey.

Diop, C. A. (1974). *The African origin of civilization: Myth or reality?* Lawrence Hill.

Diop, C. A. (1981). *Civilisation ou barbarie*. Presence Africaine.

Du Bois, W. E. B. (1989). *The souls of Black folk*. Bantam.

Fanon, F. (1963). *The wretched of the earth*. Grove.

Freire, P. (1990). *Pedagogy of the oppressed*. Continuum.

Gates, H. L. (1991, September 23). Beware of the new pharaohs: Afrocentricity and education. *Newsweek, 118*(13), 47.

Gramsci, A. (1949). *Note sul Machiavelli, sulla politica, e sullo stato moderno* [Notes on Machiavelli, politics, and the modern state]. Einaudi.

Harris, N. (1992). A philosophical basis for an Afrocentric orientation. *Western Journal of Black Studies, 16*(3), 154–159.

Hilliard, A. G., III, Payton-Stewart, L., & Obadele Williams, L. (Eds.). (1990). *Infusion of African and African American content in the school curriculum: Proceedings of the first National Conference*. Aaron.

hooks, b. (1990). *Yearning: Race, gender, and cultural politics*. South End.

Karenga, M. (1967). *The quotable Karenga*. Kawaida Publications.

Karenga, M. (1980). *Kawaida theory: An introductory outline*. Kawaida Publications.

Karenga, M. (1982). *Introduction to Black studies*. University of Sankore Press.

Karenga, M. (1984). *Selections from the Husia: Sacred wisdom of ancient Egypt*. Sankore.

Karenga, M. (1988). Black studies and the problematic of paradigm: The philosophical dimension. *Journal of Black Studies*, 18(4), 395–414.

Keto, C. T. (1989). *The Africa-centered perspective of history*. K. A.

Lincoln, C. E., & Mumiya, L. H. (1990). *The Black church in the African American experience*. Duke University Press.

Newsum, H. E. (1990). *Class, language education: Class struggle and sociolinguistics in an African situation*. Africa World Press.

Nobles, W. W. (1985). *Africanity and the Black family*. Black Family Institute.

Oyebade, B. (1990). African studies and the Afrocentric paradigm: A critique. *Journal of Black Studies*, 21(2), 233–238.

Perry, B. (Ed.). (1989). *Malcolm X: The last speeches*. Pathfinder.

T'Shaka, 0. (1990). *The art of leadership*. Pan Afrikan Publications.

Steele, S. (1990). *The content of our character*. St. Martin's.

Weber, M. (1958). *The Protestant ethic and the spirit of capitalism*. Scribner.

West, C. (1982). *Prophesy deliverance: An Afro-American revolutionary Christianity*. Westminster.

10.
Cabral, Black liberation and cultural struggle

In this chapter I reflect on Amilcar Cabral's influence on revolutionary Black nationalist theory in the USA in the early 1970s. Paying particular attention to two speeches made by Cabral—"The weapon of theory", given in Havana, Cuba, in 1966 and "National liberation and culture", given at Syracuse University in the USA in 1970—I focus on the Revolutionary Action Movement's House of Umoja (RAM/HOU) as representative of revolutionary Black nationalist thought and practice during that time.

I became an activist in the Black liberation movement in the USA as a young university student in 1972 just one year prior to the death of Amilcar Cabral. As I was drawn into the movement, it was Cabral, Malcolm X and Frantz Fanon whose names, images and ideas were most prominent in shaping my early political development. These three giants were most influential in the development of the revolutionary Black nationalist theory and practice that was the root and grounding of my life and continued to be a tremendous influence four decades later.

Malcolm was seminally important to linking Black nationalism and African American people to the burgeoning anticolonial struggles of the time. At the same time, Fanon was key in demonstrating through his writing and his practical commitment what Black internationalism looked like. However, it was from Cabral that revolutionaries learnt how to build a practical revolutionary theory from their own experience and cultural context. It is from Cabral that the Black liberation movement learnt that revolutionary struggle must be pragmatic and that it must be ruthlessly self-critical in its assessment of the struggle in the context of real situations. Cabral's (1969) axiom "tell no lies, claim no easy victories ..." became for thousands of young nationalists in the United States both a warning and a guiding principle of how to wage a revolutionary struggle.

These and other ideas of Cabral were very important to the development of *revolutionary Black nationalism,* as espoused by the Revolutionary Action Movement's House of Umoja, which was the movement organisation through which I began my activist career. Cabral's ideas on national liberation and culture, in particular, and the relationship of cultural struggle to the development of a national identity against colonial oppression were very evident in the theory and practice of the revolutionary Black nationalism of the early 1970s to 1980s. In the United States, this was a particularly significant issue in that within the Black liberation movement there were contending groups promoting *cultural nationalism,* as espoused by the Us Organization, on the one hand, and a *non-culturalist intercommunalism,* as espoused by the Black Panther Party for Self Defense (BPPSD), on the other hand. Kawaida, the primary theory of Black cultural nationalism as developed by Maulana Karenga (2004), posited that cultural revolution must be waged and won by Black people before political revolution was possible. Karenga argued that cultural revolution would be waged through the "rescue and reconstruction" of traditional African history and cultural practices.

Though the BPPSD initially adhered to some ideas of revolutionary Black nationalism, the party soon rejected both Black nationalism and internationalism under the theoretical direction of Huey P Newton (2006). In his theory of *revolutionary intercommunalism,* Newton argued that nations no longer existed, which would have been a surprise to Cabral. An important aspect of Newton's theory is his notion of the vanguard role of the lumpenproletariat. Newton argued that rather than the working class, the peasantry or even the petit bourgeoisie being central to building a revolutionary movement, it was in fact the pimps, prostitutes, drug dealers and so on who were the most revolutionary class in the Black liberation struggle. This argument was made with only marginal thought to the need to challenge the culture and consciousness of this class. Newton (1968) argued that cultural nationalism was reactionary and contributed to the people's oppression. He said,

> Cultural nationalism, or pork chop nationalism, as I sometimes call it, is basically a problem of having the wrong political perspective. It seems to be a reaction instead of responding to political oppression. The cultural nationalists are concerned with returning to the old African culture and thereby regaining their identity and freedom. In other words, they feel that the African culture will automatically bring political freedom. Many times cultural nationalists fall into line as reactionary nationalists. (Newton, 1968, p. 4)

These extremes in cultural analysis aided by a lack of maturity within the movement left both of these wings of the Black liberation movement extremely vulnerable to government infiltration, disinformation and disruption through the FBI's counterintelligence program (COINTELPRO), which left scores of Us Organization members and Black Panthers emotionally damaged, dead from intergroup shootouts, or languishing in prison and laying the blame on each other.

Differently from either the cultural nationalism of the Us Organization or the revolutionary intercommunalism of the Black Panther Party, the revolutionary Black nationalism of RAM/HOU, influenced by Cabral's analysis, argued that *cultural struggle* is not a distinct stage that precedes political struggle, as the cultural nationalists argued, nor is culture an issue somehow largely insignificant to how revolution is waged, as the Panthers believed. Revolutionary Black nationalists agreed with Cabral (1973, p. 43) that "national liberation is necessarily an act *of culture*". Revolutionary Black nationalism in the USA, in unity with Cabral, saw that a movement for liberation—as was waged in communities around police abuse, as was done by the Coalition Against Police Abuse (CAPA) in Los Angeles, or for workers' rights, or to challenge the legitimacy of the celebration of the US Bicentennial as the Afro-American Anti-Bicentennial Committee (AAABC) did from 1974 to 1976—was in fact a struggle for the minds and hearts of the people. Cabral (1973) wrote:

> A reconversion of minds—of mental set—is thus indispensable to the true integration of people into the liberation movement. Such reconversion—re-Africanization, in our case—may take place before the struggle, but it is complete only during the course of the struggle, through daily contact with the popular masses in the communion of sacrifice required by the struggle. (Cabral, 1973 p. 45)

Rather than imagining that cultural analysis was something unimportant to and distinct from political struggle, or that cultural revolution somehow could be waged prior to and again distinct from the political struggle, learning from Cabral, revolutionary Black nationalism understood that day-to-day political struggle around the important questions and situations of Black lived experience in fact was a process of *re-Africanization* and creating a national identity of Black people distinct from the colonising American identity under which they were oppressed. They agreed with Cabral that "History proves that it is much less difficult to dominate and to continue dominating a people whose culture is similar or analogous to that of the conqueror" (1973 p. 48). When day-to-day political struggle is engaged in *acts of culture,* it becomes clear that culture is not about recreating ancient African traditions from all around the African continent (though these traditions may be helpful in redefining African identity) or about creating rigid definitions of what is or is not African. Cabral, like Fanon, believed that culture, understood as revolutionary action, was a living, dialectical force within society. Cabral (1973) wrote:

> Culture, like history is an expanding and developing phenomenon. Even more important, we must take account of the fact that the fundamental characteristic of a culture is the highly dependent and reciprocal nature of its linkages with the social and economic reality of the environment, with the level of productive forces and the mode of production or the society which created it. (Cabral, 1973, p. 50)

In other words, unlike some cultural nationalists, Cabral and the revolutionary Black nationalists of the RAM/HOU understood that culture is under constant reconstruction and recreation and is absolutely linked to social and economic forces in society. Cabral, in an African-centred challenge to traditional Marxist materialist analysis, argued that it was not *class struggle* that was the motive force of history, but that the *productive forces* of a particular society were the motive force of history whatever the society's social structure. He argued that this understanding, unlike traditional Marxism, did not leave Africa and Africans outside of history simply because these societies did not have class structures in the manner understood by Marxists. At the same time, while challenging Marxist ideas, Cabral understood that Africans and other colonised people did not live in some antiseptic bubble outside of the realities of capitalist domination. Cabral's nationalist analysis included an analysis of capitalism and the resultant imperialism and colonialism, which impacted Africa and the rest of the Third World.

This ability to "eat the fish and spit out the bones" in his criticism of Marxist analysis was a powerful example by Cabral for revolutionary nationalists in the United States struggling to understand the situation of Black people in the USA through the lens of an authentic African-centred worldview that allowed the Black liberation movement to maintain a connection with the worldwide anticolonial and anticapitalist struggles of other Third-World peoples.

Cabral (1969) in fact argued that the great moral contradiction of imperialism and colonialism is that these systems deny oppressed peoples their *self-agency* or, as revolutionary nationalists argue, *self-determination*:

> We therefore see that both in colonialism and in neo-colonialism the essential characteristic of the imperialist domination remains the same: the negation of the historical process of the dominated people by means of violent usurpation of the freedom of development of the national productive forces. (Cabral, 1969, p. 102)

What Cabral is arguing here is that oppression stunts colonised people's self-agency (self-determination) by denying them control of their own productive forces, whether that be land, labour or tools. In effect, colonialism, by exploiting the land, labour and wealth of the colonised, denies them control of their own historical destiny and development. He says that this is a *negation* of the oppressed people's historical process. By extension, a revolutionary struggle for national liberation "rejects the negation of its historical process". This is truly what Marxists would call a *negation of the negation*.

This leaves us with the question, what can Black activists learn from Amilcar Cabral today, 40 years after his untimely death? As of this writing, Barack Obama has just won re-election for a second term as president of the United States. What the first four years exposed was that despite liberals' and conservatives' wishful thinking that his election would bring in an era of *post-racial* enlightenment, the election of the first African American president has only exposed the still-festering white supremacist leanings of a significant section of the American population. As the country struggled to salvage the economy, even as the unemployment rate improved overall ever so slightly, it remained largely unchanged for African Americans at around 14%, twice the national rate. Several high-profile deaths of African American youths like Trayvonne Martin and Michael Brown exposed the reality that every 28 hours, a Black person is killed by the police or some other representative of the state in the USA. On the international front, as the war in Afghanistan has raged on, the US policy of imperial domination through military might has been magnified by the Obama administration, most profoundly demonstrated through assassinations and killing of both foreign and domestic-born combatants by American drones. Queen Mother Audley Moore, an early revolutionary Black nationalist leader and a mentor of Malcolm X (see Farmer, 2025), was known for saying "you might not think you are *at war*, but whether you like it or not you are *in* a war". This seems to be the situation with not just African Americans, but as the US capitalist system has hardened, with other communities of people in the USA as well. In this light, it is clear to me that many of Cabral's lessons on culture and the revolutionary situation are pertinent and useful today.

Finally, Cabral encouraged a pragmatic approach to national liberation struggle. That practicality also influenced the revolutionary Black nationalism of the RAM/HOU and other organisations. Through pragmatism as opposed to dogmatism, movements are able to survive even the worst of onslaughts. It was understood that theory is critical to successful national liberation struggles; however, theory that is not self-critical and open to being tested is simply ideology. While it may seem that revolutionary theory and practice has declined in the USA, especially within the African American communities, there is a front of stiff resistance in urban centres around the USA. Young people, workers and organisers are rebuilding and learning lessons about organising through these past difficult years. It is certainly the lessons and legacy of martyrs and heroes like Amilcar Cabral which will contribute to the re-emerging liberation movements of the 21st century in the United States.

References

Cabral, A. (1966). *The weapon of theory*. Color Collective.

Cabral, A. (1969). Tell no lies claim no easy victories... In R. Handyside (Ed.), *Revolution in Guinea: Selected texts by Amilcar Cabral* (pp. 70–72). Monthly Review Press

Cabral, A. (1973). National liberation and culture. In Africa Information Service (Ed.), *Return to the Source: Selected Speeches of Amilcar Cabral* (pp. 39–55). Monthly Review Press.

Farmer, A.D. (2025) *Queen Mother: Black nationalism, reparations, and the untold story of Audley Moore*. Pantheon.

Karenga, M. (2004). *Kawaida theory: An African communitarian philosophy*. Kawaida Publishers.

Newton, H. P. (1968). An interview with Huey P. Newton. In Students for a Democratic Society (Ed.), *Huey Newton talks to the movement about the Black Panther Party, cultural nationalism, SNCC, liberals and white revolutionaries* (pp. 4–14). Students for a Democratic Society.

Newton, H. P. (2006). Intercommunalism. In A. Gdala (Ed.), *Revolutionary intercommunalism and the right of nations to self-determination*, (pp. 21–32). Cyhoeddwyr y Superscript.

11.
Culture is the heartbeat of revolution

A speech by Makungu Akinyela for the National Malcolm X Assassination Commemoration, February 2022.

Many years ago, in the early years of my own participation in our people's struggle for self-determination, I along with my brother Akinyele Umoja had the opportunity to visit our sister comrade Afeni Shakur in her small apartment in Oakland, California. Afeni, along with Dr Mutulu Shakur, was coordinating the COINTELPRO Research and Litigation Taskforce designed to expose and dismantle the US government attempt to disrupt and destroy our movement through its counterintelligence program. While that meeting was many years ago and I don't remember a lot of details about a lot of our conversation, Afeni said something at that time stemming from our discussion about the current situation and the time we were in. Afeni said, "This is the first time in our movement when we have not had a song. When we have not had music to carry us through the struggle". Then I remember she began to lament all of her lost comrades. Some were dead. But since the heady days of intense revolution in the

1960s and early 70s, many were now struggling with alcoholism and drug addiction, mental illness and alienation from their families. And Afeni told us that she believed that much of that pain and hurt and disruption was because we had lost our cultural and artistic centre. There was no revolutionary culture to light our way.

That conversation affected me and stuck with me as I looked around the struggle at that time and saw how right she was. There was lots of activity, but it seemed to be soulless and without direction. Though she may not have used these words, Sister Afeni was teaching us that "culture is the heartbeat of revolution". I know that a lot of people listening tonight might agree with that thought, but it's important to remember that that has not always been an agreed-on supposition.

Another respected elder comrade, Brother Askia Muhammad Touré, in a separate conversation, once reminded me that between the anti-African culture position of the Oakland-based Black Panther Party for Self Defense and the cultural nationalism of the Los Angeles–based Us Organization, there was a third perspective on culture and its role in our struggle as provided by the revolutionary Black nationalism of the Revolutionary Action Movement. And I need to make clear that as a mass movement, not all members of MXGM (the Malcolm X Grassroots Movement) have moved to the political position of revolutionary Black nationalism, but nevertheless, MXGM stands proudly in the political lineage of the Revolutionary Action Movement as it was shaped by Malcolm X, Queen Mother Audley Moore and Robert F Williams. Differently from either the cultural nationalism of the Us Organization or the revolutionary intercommunalism of the Black Panther Party, the revolutionary Black nationalism of RAM, influenced by Amilcar Cabral's analysis, argued that cultural struggle is not a distinct stage that precedes the political struggle, as the cultural nationalists argued, nor is culture an issue somehow largely insignificant to how revolution is waged, as the Panthers believed. Revolutionary Black nationalists agreed with Cabral (1973, p. 43) that "national liberation is necessarily an act of culture". Revolutionary Black nationalism in the USA, in unity with Cabral, saw that as a movement for liberation was waged in communities around police or for workers' rights or to challenge the legitimacy of American political holidays like the fourth of July, it was in fact a struggle for the minds and hearts of the people. Cabral (1973) wrote:

> A reconversion of minds—of mental set—is thus indispensable to the true integration of people into the liberation movement. Such reconversion—re-Africanization, in our case—may take place before the struggle, but it is complete only during the course of the struggle, through daily contact with the popular masses in the communion of sacrifice required by the struggle. (Cabral, 1973, p. 45)

Rather than imagining that cultural analysis was something unimportant to and distinct from political struggle, or that cultural revolution somehow could be waged prior to and again distinct from the political struggle, learning from Cabral, revolutionary Black nationalism understood that day-to-day political struggle around the important questions and situations of Black lived experience was in fact a process of re-Africanization and creating a national identity of Black people distinct from the colonising American identity under which they were oppressed. Revolutionary Black nationalists agreed with Cabral that "History proves that it is much less difficult to dominate and to continue dominating a people whose culture is similar or analogous to that of the conqueror" (1973, p. 48). When day-to-day political struggle is engaged in acts of culture, it becomes clear that culture is not about recreating ancient African traditions from all around the African continent (though these traditions may be helpful in redefining African identity) or about creating rigid definitions of what is or is not African. Cabral, like Fanon, believed that culture, understood as revolutionary action, was a living dialectical force within society. Cabral wrote:

> Culture, like history, is an expanding and developing phenomenon. Even more important, we must take account of the fact that the fundamental characteristic of a culture is the highly dependent

and reciprocal nature of its linkages with the social and economic reality of the environment, with the level of productive forces and the mode of production or the society which created it. (1973, p. 50)

In other words, unlike some cultural nationalists, Cabral and the revolutionary Black nationalists of the RAM understood that culture is under constant reconstruction and recreation and is absolutely linked to social and economic forces in society. When Sister Afeni Shakur made that lament over 35 years ago, she was hitting on a real truth! When people have a consciously African culture that separates itself from the culture of our oppressors; and when they have traditions, rituals, observations and holidays that consciously contradict the propaganda of the coloniser; and when we have artists who produce art that is grounded solidly in the rhythm and the beat of our African culture of resistance, self-reliance and self-determination; that culture begins to shape a new identity: a national identity and a revolutionary identity.

As we continue to wage this fight for human rights, against genocide and for reparations, we need some music to inspire us to move on up and keep on pushing! We need dances to inspire us to keep fighting to free our political prisoners and prisoners of war. We need poetry that reminds us that women hold up half the sky and that our fight is to free the whole Black nation whatever its gender or sexuality expression.

We need games we can play that teach our children how to fight to defend the nation, and we need hairstyles and dress styles that scream our defiance against American colonialism and white supremacy! If we are going to keep up this fight to free the land, we need a revolutionary Black nationalist African resistance culture that moves us to dance and sing and celebrate while we demonstrate and strike and defend ourselves and make ourselves ungovernable by our coloniser. Culture is the heartbeat of revolution, and though back those 30-something years ago it might have looked like we had lost heart, I believe that this new generation of New Afrikans are showing us that they know how to make a Black nation rise.

Agitate. Educate. Organise.

12.
Cultural resistance when the house is burning

David Denborough: The pieces in this section about cultural struggle seem vitally relevant to the present day. The current crisis in the USA (and beyond US borders) is in many ways a struggle over culture. A white supremacist, Christian nationalist version of culture is being asserted, and all other versions of culture and cultural institutions are under assault. I'm keen to hear your ideas about cultural struggle now.

Makungu Akinyela: Yes. The growing fascist movement is certainly intent on denying or eliminating our culture. The anti-DEI (diversity, equity and inclusion) drive of the fascists, for instance, is clearly aimed at cultural domination rooted in white supremacist mythologies. In this situation, and always, culture is a shield we use for the defence of our lives and a means to fight for decolonisation and freedom.

What we are finding with this assault on our culture and our being is that our people's resolve and sense of collective identity is sharpening. There's a popular saying among Black folks right now: "Nobody's coming to save us". This doesn't mean that people have given up hope, but instead, our people are saying we've got to do the work ourselves. It means that Black self-reliance is essential at this time. We've got to increase our own self-reliance, our own sense of self-determination.

Are there particular historic moments in cultural struggle that you are remembering and calling on at this time?

Yes, in some ways this is similar to the early days of the Black Power movement and the Black Arts Movement. That was a time when people were responding to the intensity of the racist resistance to the civil rights movement, a movement that was grounded in the idea that at some point Black people could be integrated and included into the larger society. When we saw intense violent racist resistance to this idea of integration, the Black Power movement began to argue against prioritising inclusion and towards building our own institutions to determine our own destinies. At one time, Dr Martin Luther King said to Harry Belafonte, "I am of the suspicion that we're … integrating into a burning house" (Belafonte, 2017). I think it's a similar time now. The house is burning.

Can you say more about the Black Arts Movement and how it may be relevant to these times?

Both the Black Power movement and the Black Arts Movement emerged in the 1960s when our people began to reject the idea that the only road to freedom for us was to be integrated into a "burning house". Rather than protesting against or reaching out towards our oppressors to call to be included, instead we began to sing praises of ourselves and of our own possibilities. This was not based on hopelessness, but instead ignited a real, regained energy.

The Black Arts Movement was the soul or spirit of Black Power. One of the most important things to come out of this movement was the Black aesthetic and the idea of "Black is beautiful". It also redefined the meaning of art and declared that all art has to have a purpose. There's no such thing as art for art's sake. The Black aesthetic instead called for an art that is revolutionary, that is geared towards transforming society. Those who shaped this tradition included Amiri Baraka (LeRoi Jones), Sonia Sanchez and later Toni Morrison (see Jones & Neal, 1968).

All these voices began to redefine what our culture is and to use our culture as both a shield and a weapon of liberation. It's hard to describe just how significant the Black Arts Movement was in our struggle for resistance, for freedom, and for the development of what Frantz Fanon referred to as a national consciousness (1963, pp. 148–205). Fanon described how culture is sharpened and developed through revolutionary struggle and resistance. I agree with Fanon that to hold on to and defend and express national culture for oppressed people is a political act of resistance. Politics cannot be waged outside of cultural context, and culture in the face of political oppression is itself political. It's in the struggle to survive and the struggle towards freedom that colonised people become differently aware of themselves as a people. The Black Arts Movement transformed how so many of us understood ourselves.

You mention you see some similarities emerging now in this time of crisis?

What we're finding with this renewed assault on our culture is that our people's resolve and collective sense of identity as a people is once again sharpening, not unlike what happened in the 1960s. It's not big right now; people are rocked and trying to find ways forward. But if you understand the moves of culture and the moves of consciousness, I think you can see certain streams that are beginning to come together, and this includes renewed forms of cultural resistance.

Black people are rising to the defence of our culture. All month people have been fervently singing the Black national anthem—Lift every voice and sing—and paying more attention to our cultural practices and our rituals that define us as a people. For instance, we're giving new power and new meaning to Black History Month. We also see a kind of rising cultural resistance in people wearing their natural hair and African-centred dress. I've also been surprised at how boldly some folks are reclaiming our dialect and speaking through what I call our mother language of Ebonics even in white spaces. Ebonics is the language African American people speak, and I hear it more boldly these days even in the business room or the office. Whereas before we would code switch, now people are more boldly saying, "This is the way I talk, in whatever environments I am in".

These are all efforts to assert our culture and identity as a form of resistance to white domination as it is being exerted by the MAGA fascist movement. I think this is symbolic of people turning towards our culture and holding on to it as a defence against aggression.

In Chapter 11 of this book, you describe how culture has always been a heartbeat of the revolution. At this time, is culture also a heartbeat?

Our culture is a heartbeat and a shield and a weapon. And when the house is burning, we hear it as a heartbeat, we hold it as a shield, and we use it as resistance.

References

Belafonte, H. (2017, April 10). *Harry Belafonte interview: A friendship with MLK that shaped history* (Taylor Branch, interviewer) [Video]. YouTube. https://www.youtube.com/watch?v=2mGQ8fd_JH8

Fanon, F. (1963). *The wretched of the earth.* Grove.

Jones, L., & Neal, L. (Eds.) (1968). *Black fire: An anthology of Afro-American writing.* Morrow.

Part four:
Education as freedom

Education as freedom

There were two demands that Africans first made after the end of slavery in the United States: one for land and one for education. They wanted land and they wanted to be taught to "read, write and cipher", which had been illegal under slavery. They saw education as a source of power. African American liberatory education has always been about freedom and democracy.

There is a very rich tradition that flows from the early Freedmen's Schools, which were set up for the freed enslaved people, to the work of Carter G Woodson in the 1920s and 1930s, who, through his book *The Mis-education of the Negro* (Woodson, 2017), critiqued how education systems were serving oppression and who developed alternative educational protocols and pedagogy and associations to educate Black people for their own freedom. It flows from the citizenship schools of the 1950s, in which Septima Clark and Ella Baker began to teach Black people reading, writing and arithmetic in order to prepare them to register to vote, through to the 1960s, when the Black Panther Party and the Republic of New Afrika and other Black nationalist groups developed what were called Independent Freedom Schools. The history of Black education has always been a liberatory history.

Today in the United States, Black education, indeed all public education, is under direct threat. As part of an authoritarian grab for power, efforts are underway to drastically limit if not abolish public education. Now more than ever, the learnings from African American liberatory education seem crucial.

The way I understand critical pedagogy is that the purpose of education should be focused on giving students an experience of freedom in the classroom, as opposed to giving students an experience of domination and oppression. The aim is to create contexts in which students can talk about and problematise areas of life and which challenge students to figure out ways to create a different world. A secondary purpose of liberatory education is to give students the experience of living in a democratic liberated system so when they become challenged by oppressors, they won't accept their oppression.

In this section of this book there are three pieces. The first is about the significance of African-centred critical pedagogy. The second tells a story of the use of African-centred critical pedagogy to value everyday resistance witnessed in Black family life. And the third, entitled "Fugitive pedagogies", considers responses to the contemporary assault on education.

Reference

Woodson, C. G. (2017). *The mis-education of the negro* (T. Darnell, Ed.). 12th Media Services.

13.

*Education as an experience of freedom:
African-centred critical pedagogy
and social justice*

I am very interested in pedagogy and methodologies of teaching as they relate to Black families and students. Critical pedagogy speaks not only to the *methodologies* of teaching, but to the entire process of education and human development, which occurs both inside and outside of school settings and teaching situations.

Critical pedagogy is concerned with how humans learn within the social, political and cultural context of their environment. Therefore, the daily lived experiences of individuals in Black communities are pedagogical experiences that shape consciousness, define culture and set the parameters of community. Critical pedagogy is particularly concerned with the developmental process that occurs within unequal power relationships in society (Darder, 2012; Freire, 2000), and how these unequal power relationships affect the ability of the oppressed to develop and exist as full and free human beings in the world.

Freire (2000) and others (Darder, 2012; Giroux, 1989; Freire & Shor, 1987) have posited that oppressive pedagogy serves the purpose of perpetuating unequal social relationships and exploitative conditions for the oppressed by creating a sense of acceptance of the status quo. Freire wrote:

> This phenomenon derives from the fact that the oppressed, at a certain moment of their existential experience, adopt an attitude of "adhesion" to the oppressor. Under these circumstances they cannot "consider" him sufficiently clearly to objectivize him—to discover him "outside" themselves. This does not necessarily mean that the oppressed are unaware that they are downtrodden. But their perception of themselves as oppressed is impaired by their submersion in the reality of oppression. (Freire, 2000, p. 30)

What Freire is saying is that every aspect of oppressive pedagogy, both inside and outside of schools, prepares the oppressed to *desire* to be like the oppressor and to blame *themselves* for their subordinate position in society, rather than preparing them to question their oppression or to challenge the morality of their social condition.

Critical pedagogy posits that traditional Western pedagogy is education that is developed *for* not *with* the oppressed. Freire identified critical pedagogical education as cultural action for freedom (1985). Therefore, education is a profoundly political act that should be directed towards strengthening the oppressed. Freire (1993, p. 40) wrote that "the fundamental issue is politics. It has to do with which content gets taught, to whom, in favor of what, of whom, against what, against whom, and how it gets to be taught". Education is always in the interest of some segment of society, which may be defined by race, class, gender or any number of classifications. Both teachers and students also bring along certain presumptions, ideas, cultural beliefs and values into the learning situation, which influences what is actually learnt.

Traditional Western education, whether it is conservative or liberal, accepts and works out of the assumption of educational neutrality and the fundamental superiority of Western (European) capitalist society. European superiority and domination in relationship to educational neutrality can have devastating psychological impact on people whose primary culture is other than European. This is a critical point posed by

Antonia Darder (2012) in her studies on the development and education of bicultural children. She wrote:

> Both these views [conservative and liberal] essentially uphold the notion that the object of education [i.e. the ideal student] is the free, enterprising, independent individual, and that students should be educated in order to adapt to the existing configurations of power that make up the dominant society. (Darder, 2012, p. 20)

When one assumes that education serves all learners and teachers equally, issues of power, prejudice and privilege in the society and in the classroom are rarely confronted, though these issues profoundly affect the lives of both students and teachers. The basic inequality in society is reproduced in the classroom. Students are rarely encouraged to question their relationships to the social order, the economic structure of society or the asymmetrical social relationships that exist between themselves and their oppressors. The very denial or failure to speak to contradictions and power differentials, and their implications and effects in the classroom, is in itself an oppressive political act of control.

Freire (1990) used several metaphors to describe methods of teaching that are derived from oppressive assumptions about education. One form of oppressive teaching is "banking". A fundamental aspect of banking is its narrative character. Teachers "narrate" the content of subjects to be learnt, while students are expected to listen passively to the "stories" that the teachers weave in the learning process. Freire (1990) wrote that the teacher's task is:

> to "fill" the students with the contents of his narration—contents which are detached from reality, disconnected from the totality that engendered them and could give them significance ... Narration (with the teacher as narrator) leads the students to memorize mechanically the narrated content. Worse yet, it turns them into "containers", into "receptacles" to be "filled" by the teacher. The more completely he fills the receptacles, the better a

teacher he is. The more meekly the receptacles permit themselves to be filled, the better students they are. (Freire, 1990, p. 57)

In the banking mode of education, the life experience and ability of the student is generally ignored. The primary objective of banking education is to reproduce the structure of the dominant society. Banking reinforces and maintains acceptable social and educational myths, which place all authority and ownership of knowledge in the hands of the teacher. Banking education identifies the "good" student as one who is passive and capable of absorbing information from the teacher and working well while being isolated from both meaningful interaction with peers and from their cultural context.

Banking education is grounded in the Eurocentric notion of the objectivity and universality of knowledge (Ani, 1994). This theory posits that knowledge (especially Western scientific knowledge) is handed down from generation to generation in an unchanged state and that this knowledge is good for all time and all people. Contrary to this notion, critical pedagogy posits that knowledge is socially constructed and culturally mediated within societies and affected by historical conditions (Darder, 2012). Human beings construct knowledge in their critical reflection on lived experiences out of which they are able to define and name their own sociopolitical reality. Darder has written of the importance of constructing knowledge from the lived histories of oppressed peoples:

> With this in mind, a critical approach must appropriate [oppressed people's] own histories by delving into their own biographies and systems of meaning ... [A] critical perspective opposes the positivist emphasis on historical continuities and linear development. In its place is found a mode of analysis that stresses the breaks, discontinuities, and tensions in history, all which become valuable in that they highlight the centrality of human agency and struggle while simultaneously revealing the gap between society as it presently exists and society as it might be. (Darder, 2012, p. 79)

The image of these "stresses and breaks" creates a "jazz" view of knowledge and cultural development. Good jazz musicians create their music between the sometimes-atonal notes, rhythms and beats of their improvised sound. The stresses, breaks, discontinuities and tensions in history are the contradictions, situations and problems to be solved between individuals and social groups. They are the rhythm or motive force of history and the locus of the construction of knowledge.

This "jazz view" challenges both the Eurocentric notion of "pure" classical knowledge, which is handed down from generation to generation, and the idea that societies can be perfected by simply reproducing old systems and traditions of knowledge. The jazz view of knowledge as particularised and socially mediated within cultures challenges the concept of knowledge as an individual pursuit preserved for the Eurocentric elite.

Pedagogy, culture and context

Critical pedagogy has made tremendous contributions towards the liberation of education from oppressive paradigms. As envisioned by Freire (1990), Freire and Shor (1987), Giroux (1989) and others, it has been useful for understanding the dynamic struggle between knowledge and power in traditional education. However, the shapers of critical pedagogy have been unable to forthrightly confront the particular issues of power as they are generated in the matrix of racism and the marginalisation of culturally subordinated ethnic groups in the USA (Akoto, 1992). It has been in the theoretical development of writers "of colour", writing out of their own cultural experience, that critical pedagogy has been able to transform itself and maintain its liberatory power.

The most significant contribution to critical pedagogy for people of colour has been Darder's theory of bicultural human development. Biculturalism is not a reference to cultural skills development (de Anda, 1984; Rashid, 1984). Bicultural identity is a psycho-social process experienced by members of a subordinate culture living within a pervasive and hostile dominant culture that devalues the content and meaning of the subordinate culture. Darder (2012, p. 45) wrote that "Biculturalism is a process wherein individuals learn to function in two distinct sociocultural environments: their primary culture and that of the dominant mainstream culture of the society in which they live". She continued, "the process of biculturation incorporates the different ways in which bicultural human beings respond to the daily struggle with racism and other forms of cultural invasion". Biculturalism is a survival response to marginalisation and an affirmation of cultural identity.

Bicultural children observe adults from their own group and similar groups who function in various ways within the society at different rates of ease and success. These ways are defined by what Darder calls "cultural response patterns" (ways of relating to the dominant culture) and "modes of engagement" (culturally moderated ways of thinking and problem-solving).

Bicultural development

Critical pedagogy theory and bicultural development theory are relevant to the situation of Black people and Black communities where the pedagogy in both formal educational settings and in daily lived experience is permeated by a lack of coherence between discourse and practice (Freire, 1993). Often teachers and other authority figures in Black communities engage in a theoretical discourse that emphasises liberatory or Afrocentric principles while their behaviour towards students supports an oppressive and authoritarian social structure.

In formal classroom settings as well as in the "classroom" of the world, teachers and others in authority in Black communities voice concerns for freedom and Black cultural self-determination while utilising oppressive and Eurocentric methods that contradict the expressed intent of their discourse. Ritualised rules that place emphasis and greater value on dress, language and the use of titles in front of names than on mutually honouring relationships send subtle and sometimes not-so-subtle messages about what is socially expected of whom.

The use of oppressive pedagogical methods by Black teachers and authority figures is an attempt by them to exert power over others within the context of a social order in which one's place in a power-driven hierarchy is essential to personal success (Freire & Faundez, 1989). In public schools in Black communities, it is not unusual for students to be disciplined for questioning the ideas of instructors or for boldly raising ideas counter to the accepted ones. Students who ask too many challenging questions, or who ask in a contradictory spirit rather than in a spirit of mere clarification, are assumed to be attacking the authority of the teacher.

The asymmetrical power relationships and authoritarian oppressive pedagogy that begins in schooling continues in the broader society. Just as students are not allowed to seriously challenge the knowledge and power of teachers, working people and the poor in the Black community are rarely permitted to challenge the status quo of the social structure.

Within the Black community itself, authoritarian lines of oppression are reproduced along colour, class and gender lines (Baer et al., 1992; Russell et al., 1992, pp. vii, 200). As a result of this dynamic of social inequality, Black communities are adversely affected both from without by daily onslaughts of institutional racism and from within by the structures, customs and pedagogical practices of Blacks in authority, which reinforce the system of racial colonialism in the Black community.

Connectedness, critical consciousness and pedagogy

Oppressive pedagogy, by its nature, is an attempt to deny the oppressed the ability to challenge the validity of their own oppression. Oppressive pedagogy is essential to cultural hegemony over the lives of the oppressed (Gramsci, 1983). Hegemony is exerted by both what is allowed in the cultural discourse and what is discouraged or muted from the discourse. When ideas are discounted, denied or ignored, possibilities and alternatives are cut off. The targets of hegemony are forced to "settle" for what they are presented with and can only figure that "this is the best (country, car, economic system, solution to oppression...) there is". This is the manner in which false or uninformed consent is garnered through legitimation and delegitimation.

The main objective of American cultural hegemony is to create an assimilated society under the leadership of the Euro-American ruling class to insure the smooth running of the dominant system. When hegemonic domination of oppressed ethnicities is successful, the bicultural person experiences both personal alienation and cultural isolation. They experience a sense of depersonalisation from others around them, while at the same time experiencing a sense of being part of a collective cultural entity (the ethnic group) that is not respected or accepted as a viable and significant participant in the larger society.

Personal alienation and cultural isolation often result in the "fatalism and apathy" that Freire reported in his first peasant students (Freire, 1983). The oppressed who experience this alienation and isolation may seem to display an inappropriate affect as they tell about the conditions of their lives. A woman may show no emotion as she describes the death of her child, or a man may seem braggadocios as he reports on his multiple children by multiple women for whom he is unable to adequately care.

According to Freire (in Freire & Faundez, 1989), the aim of creating a critical pedagogical environment is *critical consciousness*. Critical consciousness is a process, and not an end in itself. This is not simple consciousness raising or awareness. It is also not to be equated with the psychoanalytic concept of insight. Simply comprehending the objective facts of an oppressive situation or a negative set of behaviours is not enough. Critical pedagogical theory posits that as people learn to question and challenge their conditions of life, they learn to experience themselves as subjects and to comprehend the significance of their own subjectivity to the construction of knowledge about the "objective" world.

Critical consciousness can occur when students move through directed dialogues with each other and their teachers and proceed from objective awareness of reality to subjectively becoming part of the transformation of reality. It is in this dialectic at the crossroads between the objective observation of reality and the subjective experience of changing reality that knowledge or learning happens. This is the goal of critical pedagogy.

Critical African-centred theory will have some divergent views on the process. The critical pedagogy of Freire, Giroux, Short and others is a pedagogy of liberation. However, it remains a pedagogy that is centred in a worldview dependent on European psychological and cultural models. The European cultural view is evident from the dichotomous relationship between humans and nature to the point of emphasising that a major goal of critical consciousness is a recognition in the human of their distinction from and control over (ability to transform) nature.

Anthropologist Marimba Ani (1994) has argued that this dichotomy between humans and nature, with humans as subject and nature as object, is central to the destructive nature of Eurocentric philosophy, which has led to such disastrous situations as the crisis of the industrial destruction of vast portions of the Earth's ecology. When humans view the world around us as comprised of "things" to be known—that is, when all that is not human is objectified—it becomes difficult to witness the world "outside" of humanity as connected to humanity in a common creation.

Critical African-centred theory emphasises the goal of human beings becoming cognizant of their connectedness to and active participation in the process of nature. Critical African-centred theory identifies personal alienation and cultural isolation as the fundamental contradictions that create the sense of imbalance and disconnectedness within people whose primary cultural cognitive style is relational or "field sensitive" (Darder, 2012; Ramirez & Castaneda, 1974). The goal of pedagogy in the critical African-centred context is *connectedness* to community more so than individual consciousness, though of course it is recognised that this is a part of the process.

At their most conscious point, bicultural human beings act relationally in the world, aware of their connectedness to all other beings and things in the environment. Connectedness to environmental conditions, sociohistorical situations, challenges of nature or psycho-spiritual change is the source of community knowledge. Using information gained from "old community knowledge", individuals reflect, share and strive to understand as a community.

In the act of challenging new situations and problems, "new community knowledge" is constructed, which will eventually itself become "old community knowledge" to be challenged by new situations. This construction, challenge and new construction of collective knowledge provide the context in which, as Fanon (2004) wrote, "each generation must out of relative obscurity, discover its mission, fulfill it or betray it" (p. 206).

The ideas of critical pedagogy are often conveyed in literary language. African-centred pedagogy moves away from literary metaphors of "readings", "transcripts" and "texts" in referring to discourses about everyday life. Text and literary-based metaphors in many ways are cultural hegemonic intrusions of Eurocentric thought into the African experience. These metaphors privilege a European literary tradition over an African oral tradition. This becomes significant when it is assumed that the deep-structure culture of Africans in America is an oral culture that is conveyed through "stories", "testimonies" and "witnessing", more so than texts and scripts. These metaphors tap more authentically into the spiritual roots and traditions of African culture in America.

With this understanding of why privileging Eurocentric literary metaphors doesn't fit a description of African culture, let us take a look at James C Scott's (1990) work on "the hidden transcript". Scott used this metaphor to describe those traditional times and spaces in which dominated peoples speak and act out their own truth. Scott sets this in opposition to the "public transcript", which is acted out between dominator and dominated. Robin Kelley (1994, p. 7) described the hidden transcript as "a dissident political culture that manifests itself in daily conversations, folklore, jokes, songs, and other cultural practices".

Scott's basic idea of dual stories—hidden and public—being told in the everyday lives of the oppressed and oppressors is helpful, and it becomes more evidently significant for understanding Black lived experience when we envision his transcripts as testimonies or stories in the oral tradition. Eugene D Genovese (1974), the prominent American historian on slavery in the United States, argued that the relationship between enslaved Africans and their white enslavers was largely "paternalistic".

This interpretation gained wide influence with its emphasis on "good" enslavers and the enslaved who, through the paternalistic relationship, were shaped in the image of their enslavers. This paternalistic relationship between enslaved Africans and white enslavers is an example of Scott's public transcript: a story about the oppressed that is accepted as truth, but that contradicts the "hidden transcript", which is the story that the oppressed tell about themselves.

The public transcripts (literary metaphor) or public testimonies (oral metaphor) that the oppressed tell about themselves among themselves comprise what Scott called the *infrapolitics* of resistance. Infrapolitics is the quiet anti-hegemonic struggle against domination, which is often seen as shiftlessness, laziness, ignorance, passive aggression or mental disorder, but is not viewed as political action in itself by oppressors or necessarily by the oppressed (Kelley, 1994; Scott, 1990).

The traditional spaces within African oral tradition from which a "hidden testimony" of Black cultural resistance to domination could be told are in the ring shouts danced in the brush arbor; the gatherings of women to cook gumbo on Friday nights; the weekly Saturday get-togethers at corner barber shops and beauty salons; the canning parties and quilting bees. These have been the cultural pedagogical equivalents to the literacy classes of Paulo Freire or the community college courses of Ira Short. These are the spaces in which Black people could historically tell their own stories, safe from the critical, often dangerous, ears of white folk. In these places, Africans could testify to their truth and shape their own lives and, more often than not, fortify their opposition to white domination as they shared wisdom and knowledge that was used to live better, stronger lives as they went to "meet the man". This is an African-centred perspective on the point at which critical pedagogy becomes a challenge to traditional Western pedagogy and to the social structure of the status quo. By creating conditions in which they can begin to reflect on their situations while striving to change them from within their own cultural contexts, the oppressed will be able to create sites of strength and resistance to cultural and social domination.

An African-centred pedagogy will focus on creating spaces for Black people to reflect on and build on the central organising theme of resistance and resilience and the motivational cultural value of self-determination. These organising themes and cultural values are not new. They are dynamics that have been critical to the historical development of Black institutions and in the formation of Black community and Black identity.

Africana studies and social change

I am an instructor in Africana studies (also known as African American studies or Black studies), a discipline that has always been linked with not only scholarship in the purely academic sense but with social change and movements to achieve it. Most scholars of Africana studies tend to agree that there is a close link between the study of African people, history and society throughout the diaspora and the social, political and cultural conditions that make the development of such studies necessary. Since the inception of the first Black studies departments on college campuses in the 1960s, much attention has been paid to *what* is taught in Black studies and to ensuring the development of a relevant and effective curriculum. On the other hand, it seems that little attention has been paid to how Black studies is taught and the relationship of process to the effectiveness of content in curriculum. The project of building an African-centred curriculum must include a critique of traditional pedagogy and the introduction of a pedagogy of freedom; that is, a critical pedagogy. This pedagogy would be focused on integrating scholarship with action and democratising the relationship between teachers and students through a dialogical process.

I believe that the inclusion of dialogue about the *process* of pedagogy is critical if we are to conceptualise the education of Black students as part and parcel of the overall struggle of Africans in America for social, political and cultural liberation. An African-centred critical pedagogy would be aimed at providing an experience of democracy and self-determination in the classroom for students as they research and study about the efforts to attain democratic rights, self-determination and freedom for Africans in the world.

Eurocentric pedagogy

Since the first Africans illegally learnt and taught other Africans to read and write on southern plantations, Black education has been subversive and counter-hegemonic in its relationship to the American academy. The founding of various Black studies departments was based in the conscious decisions of Black students to refuse to allow education to continue "as usual". Many of these new departments created through student insurgency and rebelliousness were also committed to a democratic ideal of shared power between students and teachers, and to mutual dependence and commitment from students and teachers on the learning process and on the survival and growth of the departments. Many of these programs and departments also included strong commitment and connection to the ongoing struggles for liberation and democracy being fought in the African communities near the university campuses. For a short period on these campuses, an atmosphere of excitement, expectation, dialogue and freedom existed, all within the context of a democratic dialogue about freedom. The Black studies community often looked and felt radically different from the surrounding Eurocentric academic community in which it was embedded, adding to the sense of subversion and counter-hegemonic action in everyday experience.

In the years since that time of initial excitement and experimentation, departments of African American studies have blossomed on campuses throughout the USA, including on historically Black campuses. As these departments have become staid and permanent fixtures in the academic arena, the character, content and commitment of many of them have changed and become less distinguishable from the surrounding Eurocentric academic departments and disciplines. What I am most concerned about today is the pedagogy that guides the teaching and learning of the discipline of Africana studies and the education of Black students in general.

Often when African-centred scholars discuss Eurocentricity, we focus on the content of the curriculum; that is, on what has historically been taught about Africa and Africans from the viewpoint and in the interests of European domination of African peoples. While there has been a lot of critique of this content, there has been little discussion about the context and structure of the curriculum and the relationship dynamics engendered by this context and structure. This context and structure can be understood as the *hidden curriculum* of Eurocentric education. This hidden curriculum is defined by three characteristics among others. First there is its focus on monological lectures; second, its reliance on standardised tests (true/false, multiple choice) as the primary method of assessing student knowledge; and third, its isolation of subject matter and curriculum content from the everyday lived experience of students. The hidden curriculum includes the symbolic meanings, values and assumptions embedded in the architecture, room design and even decorations of the school and classroom, which reinforce dominant and subordinate relations of power. This hidden curriculum is embedded within the African-centred curriculum of some of our Black studies programs and the general curriculum of historically Black colleges and universities, creating a European counterinsurgency against our own efforts at changing the paradigm in Black education. This hidden curriculum includes several assumptions, both spoken and unspoken, about the relationship between students and teachers. These include the ideas that:

1. the teacher teaches and the students are taught

2. the teacher knows everything about the subject and the students know nothing

3. the teacher "thinks" and the students are "thought about"

4. the teacher talks and the students listen meekly

5. the teacher chooses the curriculum content and the students (who are never consulted) adjust to it

6. the teacher is the subject of the learning process and the students are mere objects.

The first task of the teacher in traditional education is to control the classroom. Students are rarely encouraged to question their own relationships to the social order, the economic structure of society, or the unequal relationships that exist between themselves and others. When educators deny or ignore the social problems and power differences between students and society and in the classroom, this is in itself an act of bias and an attempt to control the reality and perception of everyday life of their students.

Teaching and learning as vital dynamic

While traditional pedagogy in the college classroom is influenced by the hidden curriculum of control and domination of students by teachers, critical pedagogy strives for a dynamic reciprocity between students and teachers. In this dynamic reciprocal relationship, teachers are also students open to new learning experiences and willing to be taught by their students as experts and teachers in their own right.

Dialogue as the centre of education

As I mentioned earlier, there is tremendous history of knowledge development out of communal interaction in the cultural tradition of Africans in America. This interaction has been best demonstrated in what I call the "hidden testimony".

In my own efforts to utilise a critical pedagogical approach, I have focused on several methods that I believe are essential to providing an experience of freedom and democracy in the classroom in the tradition of the hidden testimony. First, I believe that dialogue, as the primary tool of teaching, is critical. Second, I have instituted the creation of "reflection circles" within the classroom. Third, I have instituted action-oriented learning experiences that take students out of the classroom to become their own experts on the object of study. Fourth, students are encouraged to participate in a group project along with other members of their reflection circle, once again taking their theory into the community and testing it in the field.

Dialogue

With dialogical education, the emphasis is on "asking the question" even more than having an answer. Patricia Hill Collins has argued that "the use of dialogue has deep roots in an African based oral tradition and in African American culture" (Collins, 2003, p. 59). In dialogical education, the primary role of the teacher is to raise critical questions about the subject being studied and to facilitate the flow of discussion to ensure that students are not simply focused on directing answers to the teacher, but that students become involved in a community discussion and exchange of ideas with each other.

Reflection circles

The circle is an important insurgent teaching tool against traditional pedagogy. Used properly, it is in direct opposition to the rank-and-file desk arrangement of the traditional classroom or lecture hall. The Eurocentric ideology of domination and subordination is embedded even in the physical structure of the traditional classroom. These classrooms are designed to limit students' access to each other and to keep all authority and privilege focused on the professor at the head of the class. On the other hand, the circle, which is arguably the most fundamental symbol and expression of African culture, holds great possibility for a learning experience rooted in democracy and freedom. Within the circle, students are focused on the learning community more so that on the teacher as primary authority in the learning process.

Students are often not used to being encouraged to speak their own minds about classroom subjects. Reflection circles allow students to test ideas and become involved in dialogue on specific questions in a small group. In the reflection circles, students explore questions and raise new questions about the subject being studied without the pressure of having to speak cold in front of a whole class. Once dialogue has been initiated in the small reflection circles, students are then encouraged to open up to the large circle, and to continue their dialogue by asking each other questions and making commentaries on the subject in question. This process helps students to first find and then use their voices with confidence and power.

Action-oriented learning

Action-oriented learning allows the learning process to move outside the classroom. It moves students from theory to practice so that they can return to the classroom and deepen their theory. After the first few weeks focused on diversified reading to give students information and understanding of the subject, coupled with dialogue that raises questions and helps students identify their already existing knowledge and expertise on the subject, students are encouraged to identify community resources and spaces through which they can deepen their understanding of the subject.

Group project

The group project becomes the opportunity for the students to deepen their theory even more as well as their experience of collective democratic process. This is done by using the expert information developed in action-oriented learning and applying it to the group process. Students, through their reflection circles, must decide on a collective project, work out the process of research, make contacts, hold meetings, design a multimedia presentation and collectively produce a final written project.

Problems in this process

While I believe that this approach to pedagogy is a necessary step towards developing Africana studies for the 21st century, there are several problems that must be confronted in the approach. This approach can be disconcerting to students used to the lecture, note-taking and test-taking approach to teaching and learning. It can feel unsafe and disorganised. Students also sometimes resist and resent the focus on dialogue as a central teaching method. Dialogue places much more focus and expectation on the student to read and come to the learning situation prepared. It makes it much more difficult for students to hide among the crowd. On the other hand, I have found that the majority of students who I have worked with take eagerly to this African-centred critical pedagogy and appreciate the experience of freedom and democracy in the classroom.

Conclusion

To conclude, teaching as an experience of freedom is a critical goal for Africana studies moving into the 21st century. We can no longer focus solely on what gets taught in our departments to the exclusion of how it gets taught. The quest for African liberation and self-determination is still the most important question to be addressed in African education. It still should be the goal of African studies to teach in the insurgent intellectual tradition of WEB Du Bois, Ella Baker, Septima Clark, Malcolm X, Carter G Woodson and many other African academic subversives. Our goal in Africana studies in universities, whether they are on historically Black campuses or on the campuses of European academia, should be in the tradition laid out by Mwalimu Julius Nyerere (1967), the first president of independent Tanzania. This is the tradition of "education for self-reliance". In the 21st century, self-reliance is inseparable from democracy, freedom and communitarian collective action.

References

Akoto, K. A. (1992). *Nation building: Theory and practice in Afrikan centered education.* Talking Stick.

Ani, M. (1994). *Yurugu: An African-centered critique of European cultural though and behavior.* Africa World Press.

Baer, H. A., & Jones, Y. (1992). *African Americans in the South: Issues of race, class, and gender.* University of Georgia Press.

Collins, P. H. (2003). Toward an Afrocentric feminist epistemology. In Y. S. Lincoln & N. K. Denzin (Eds.), *Turning points in qualitative research: Tying knots in a handkerchief* (pp. 47–72). AltaMira.

Darder, A. (2012). *Culture and power in the classroom: The educational foundations for bicultural education* (20th anniversary edition). Routledge.

de Anda, D. (1984). Bicultural socialization: Factors affecting the minority experience. *Social Work, 29*(2), 101–107. https://doi.org/10.1093/sw/29.2.101

Fanon, F. (2004). *The wretched of the earth.* Grove.

Freire, P. (1985). *The politics of education: Culture, power and liberation.* Bergin and Garvey.

Freire, P. (2000). *Pedagogy of the oppressed* (M. B. Ramos, Trans.) (30th anniversary ed.). Continuum.

Freire, P., & Faundez, A. (1989). *Learning to question: A pedagogy of liberation.* WCC Publications.

Genovese, E. (1974). *Roll, Jordan, roll: The world the slaves made.* Pantheon.

Giroux, H. A. (1989). *Schooling for democracy: Critical pedagogy in the modern age.* Routledge.

Gramsci, A. (1983). *Selections from the prison notebooks.* International Publishers.

Kelley, R. (1994). *Race rebels: Culture, politics, and the Black working class.* Free Press.

Nyerere, J. K. (1967). *Education for self-reliance.* Government Printer.

Ramirez, M., & Castaneda, A. (1974). *The relationship of acculturation to cognitive style among Mexican Americans.* Academic Press.

Rashid, H. M. (1984). Promoting biculturalism in young African American children. *Young Children, 39*(2), 13–23.

Russell, K. Y., Wilson, M., & Hall, R. E. (1992). *The color complex: The politics of skin color among African Americans.* Harcourt Brace Jovanovich.

Shor, I., & Freire, P. (1987). *A pedagogy for liberation: Dialogues on transforming education.* Bloomsbury Academic.

14.
Valuing everyday resistance in Black family life: A story of critical pedagogy from the university of the streets

In 1967, Dr Martin Luther King Jr published *Where Do We Go from Here: Chaos or Community?* This question is still pertinent today. In that book, Dr King attempted to highlight the contours of ideological unity between the nonviolent direct action philosophy of the civil rights movement and the fledgling ideas of revolutionary Black nationalism, which were becoming evident with the emergence of the demand for Black Power within the civil rights movement. And though some might posit that the focus of the book was aimed at critiquing the dangers inherent in a call for power unmediated by his own love ethic, I would argue that Dr King's ultimate objective in writing the book was to voice a prophetic warning. He foresaw the marginalisation of Black people to the edges of a fast-changing US society. The book was a warning against the impending chaos of free enterprise thriving on the exploitation of working and poor people as well as small wars in obscure foreign lands. Building on his well-known stand in 1967 against the war in Vietnam, in this book,

Dr King established a well thought out antiwar position that placed his opposition to the war in the context of the economic, cultural and human rights struggles of Black people in the United States.

Dr King's concern for worsening economic exploitation, intensification of ethnic hatred, racial marginalisation and weak institutions in Black communities remains as critical as ever. These conditions cited by Dr King have served as the spawning ground for the ever-growing, perpetually impoverished Black "underclass", which has largely been accepted as the non-negotiable price to be paid for social and economic progress for a privileged few among both Black and white people. The resounding response to Dr King's question seems to be that chaos has been chosen over community in American society. A critical premise of my work has been that the Black family is a cultural institution whose relational and social dynamics are influenced by a *central organising theme* of resistance and resilience against oppressive social and cultural forces in US society. This central organising theme is given meaning in Black families and other Black institutions by a desire for social, political and economic *self-determination*, which is a *motivating cultural value* for Black people in the United States as manifested through various social structures and cultural functions. Black families have navigated through various social, economic and political conditions over the centuries and exhibited the ability to transform and construct strategies of survival and resistance.

African-centred pedagogy

African-centred pedagogy (Akoto, 1992; Lee, 1994; Shujaa, 1994) places the lived experiences and cultural understanding of African descendants in the United States at the centre of social analysis of cultural and political issues that affect the lives of African people. African-centred pedagogy is a critical pedagogy that values the significance of the whole life experience as a part of the educational process. It places an emphasis on and challenges discourses of power inequality with a bias towards the oppressed and marginalised in society. This African-centred pedagogy is not limited to learning in the classroom. It is a pedagogy of liberation concerned with the learning that occurs in the "university of the streets".

Importantly, African-centred pedagogy is focused on the relationship of Black individuals and institutions as they develop within the context of a dominant European American culture and how they construct strategies of survival, resistance and sociocultural growth and development. This African-centred pedagogy is interested in the cultural strengths embedded in everyday Black life. It is also interested in Black ethos, the psycho/spiritual consciousness and sense of connectedness.

My views are indebted to the self-determinist trend of Black nationalism, which has held a consistent historical presence in the experiences of Black people. In March 1968, at the height of the Black Power movement, representatives of various militant organisations, including the Black Panther Party, Maulana Karenga's Us Organization and the League of Revolutionary Black Workers, along with such venerable personalities as Betty Shabazz, Queen Mother Audley Moore and Amiri Baraka, met in Detroit, Michigan, for the founding convention of the Republic of New Afrika. This convention was aimed at establishing an independent Black nation inside the present USA. This was one of many Black political conferences of this period and one that developed by far the most radical solution for the political problems of Black people in America. The outcome of the convention was the writing and signing of a declaration of Black independence from the United States of America. The document was signed by 100 of the 500 convention participants. Robert Williams, the former president of the Monroe North Carolina NAACP, was elected president and Betty Shabazz as vice-president of the newly formed government.

Another key document to come out of this convention was the New Afrikan Creed, a 15-point affirmation (Obadele, 1975) which read in part:

1. I believe in the spirituality, humanity and genius of black people and in our new pursuit of these values.

2. I believe in the *family* and in the *community* and *in the community as a family* and I will work to make this concept live.

3. I believe in the *community as more important than the individual.*

4. I believe in constant struggle for freedom, to end oppression and build a better world. I believe in collective struggle; in fashioning victory in concert with my brothers and sisters. (Obadele, 1975, p. 153, italics added)

The concept of connectedness between family and community expressed in this creed was a popular nationalist view of things as *they ought to be*. The concept also provides a sound paradigm for approaching the study of an institution that has been studied out of context for decades. The *Black family* has come to be associated with degradation, pathology and hopelessness, contrary to the meaning given to family if prefixed with any other ethnic/racial identification such as white family, Asian family or Latino family.

And yet, Black families are pedagogically critical institutions. Their cultural and social dynamics exhibit resistant and resilient organisational practices that are motivated by desire for collective self-determination by the Black population. African-centred pedagogical methods value the methods of resistance witnessed in everyday Black family life and count them as strengths to be built on.

Critical pedagogy as group facilitation

Many years ago, I was meeting with Black and brown parents in California, particularly those who had been court ordered to take parenting classes if they wanted to get their children back from foster care. Within my PhD, I did a class and racial analysis of this project. The foster care system and the child protective care system (now sometimes referred to as the family policing system) are gendered and racialised and put a particular focus on demonising and punishing Black and brown women.

I started off by teaching parenting classes using a curriculum that I was given. I was a young counsellor, wasn't even licensed, and I would deliver it and the participants weren't that impressed. I would give out handouts telling people how they should discipline their children, what kind of food they should feed their children, how they had to cook the balanced meals, the whole thing. I would give out these handouts, we'd have a conversation, and then I would come out after the class and the handouts had been thrown out, papers all over the school, all over the parking lot. It was a pretty clear way that the people had said, "This is bullshit". That motivated me. All through school, I had been studying critical pedagogy, but the truth is, and this is what I tell my students, I had read all of Freire's books, and I liked them, but I hadn't really understood them.

This was my chance to apply it, and it was only in my conversations with these parents that I began to understand it. Of course, Freire was teaching literacy, and this was a different context, a different kind of teaching. This was about dealing with parenting.

I spent the next several weeks with these groups of parents, not teaching them anything, but asking them questions about their lives. Asking about their experiences:

- What did they love about growing up as children?
- What did they hate about growing up as children?
- What did they love about being a parent?
- What did they hate about being a parent?

Sometimes parents were like, "Oh my god, I can't say what I hate". And I'd reply, "Of course you can say it. 'I hate this'. It's not all perfect, right? We're taught that if you're a parent and you really love your kids, you can't hate anything about it, which then makes many people feel like failures". And so, we would have all these conversations. I'd ask them to tell stories about their children. And through those conversations over several weeks, we would draw out themes, because even though it might be several different parents, there were themes that began to come up where there were similar experiences.

After spending several weeks being taught by the parents about what their lives were like, seeking to understand their lives, I had learnt a lot. And I would draw from those experiences, what Freire calls codes, and which I named as knots. In doing this, I was using a West African concept. In West African culture, an important character is the trickster. Among the Yoruba, the trickster is called Èsù who is a messenger between humans and the gods.

Besides being a messenger, Èsù also helps us to interpret life. It's Èsù who we call on to interpret and understand problematic situations. One way Èsù does this is by creating knots in our lives, like knots in a rope, which are now like a puzzle. Èsù asks us to work out how to untie this knot, how to get out of this problem. And so I would create what I call knots. These knots could be in the form of a short video or a roleplay that I created with a beginning, a middle and an end. Or it could be a drawing or a picture or a poem.

Once I had gathered all the things the parents had said to me, I represented these thematically and offered these back to them. The idea was that these knots didn't provide or give a solution, they only posed the challenge or problem to then collectively consider. Importantly, these knots were familiar to the parents because we'd talked about these things. They were familiar, but not too close. The knots were far enough away that the parents could talk about a problem without feeling that somehow the focus was on them personally.

Once I presented this knot to them, then we would go through a series of decoding questions:

- What did you see or hear?
- What's wrong with what you saw here?
- What's good about what you saw or heard?
- How might this be done differently?

We would go through this together, everyone in the circle, and everyone would contribute an idea, a reflection. What they've done is de-problematised the knot together. They've come up with ideas and practices and alternatives and I haven't taught anything. Yes, I was influential in giving some guidance, asking and answering some questions, but most of the story is constructed socially, by the group, not by an individual.

While they're talking, I write the answers, what they're saying, on a big screen or on a chart. So they're seeing their words being written, which says, "my words have significance", "What I have to say is important". And for oppressed people, this is a unique experience. Generally, their words, their thoughts, are not significant. The judge didn't listen to them. The judge just talked down to them. The judge didn't want to hear about their story. But here, their words are significant enough that we write them down, we talk about their words, we reflect on them, we ask more questions about their words, and then we come up with solutions together.

Through this process, they came up with solutions that made sense to others. We called this Ujamaa circle, a family circle. Importantly, this was also creating a community experience. One aspect of oppression, particularly in a capitalist world, is alienation and isolation. People are alienated from others and people are made to assume that you've got to fix this yourself, as opposed to having the experience of a community joining in to give support. We counter alienation and isolation through that process and give people an experience of healthy community.

The knots that we were discussing would include some of the issues that originally I was trying to "teach" in relation to disciplining their kids, or how to feed them and so on. There was an overlap between the issues the parents wanted to talk about together and those that were in the original curriculum.

For instance, the question of what to do when a child needed disciplining was certainly one of the knots. We might even show a film clip of someone yelling at a child and then going through the six questions of unknotting, deconstructing. But I was no longer an authoritarian facilitator. I was still authoritative in some way. I wanted to give people a sense that I knew what I was doing so that they had confidence in the directions we were exploring together. But I didn't want to be another authoritarian figure in the guise of authoritarian pedagogy.

Learning from the university of the streets

I can still vividly remember the image of the handouts being strewn all over the parking lot. It represents to me these parents' resistance to an authoritarian pedagogy. Their resistance in some ways set me on a new path, for which I am grateful. This was a key educational experience for me.

I began this paper with the words of Dr Martin Luther King Jr: "Where do we go from here: chaos or community?" He asked this question in 1967. Almost 60 years later, it is a question that still rings in my ears.

It's my hope that valuing everyday resistance in Black family life and using critical pedagogy to do so can play a role in our contemporary collective struggle.

References

Akoto, K. A. (1992). *Nation building: Theory and practice in Afrikan centered education*, Pan Afrikan World Institute.

King, M. L., Jr. (1967). *Where do we go from here: Chaos or community?* Harper and Row.

Lee, C. (1994). African-centered pedagogy: Complexities and possibilities. In M. J. Shujaa (Ed.), *Too much schooling, too little education: A paradox of Black life in white societies* (pp. 295–318). Africa World Press.

Obadele, I. A. (1975). *Foundations of the Black Nation: A textbook of the ideas behind the new Black nationalism and the struggle for land in America*. House of Songhay.

Shujaa, M. J. (1994). Introduction to Part 4: African centered pedagogy: An absolute necessity for African-centered education. In M. J. Shujaa (Ed.), *Too much schooling, too little education: A paradox of Black life in white societies* (pp. 265–268). Africa World Press.

15.
Fugitive pedagogies

David Denborough: Universities and schools are key sites of struggle whenever authoritarianism is on the rise.[1] This certainly seems true in the USA at this time as universities and university students are being targeted in all sorts of ways. What does education as an experience of freedom look like in your university classroom in this moment of crisis?

Makungu Akinyela: Right now, I'm teaching a course for our graduate students called "Critical pedagogy and African American education". And in this course, we're reading a book by Jarvis R Givens (2021) called *Fugitive Pedagogy: Carter G. Woodson and the Art of Black Teaching*.

This book describes a history of what they name as the "fugitive pedagogy" of African American education. In the 1920s and 1930s, during the period that Carter G Woodson lived, Black teachers around the country began to move towards his pedagogy, his teachings about Black history, Black life and society. Oftentimes they secretly taught his work in public schools where they were strictly forbidden to teach Black children about Black people's history.

The book includes the compelling story of Tessie McGee, a Black 28-year-old teaching history in 1933 and 1934 in the only Black secondary school in Webster Parish, Louisiana. She had the obligatory American history book visible and open on her desk, but she was teaching from one of Woodson's Negro history books, which was concealed on her lap under the desk. A student would sit at the door to watch out for any administrator or white person who might be coming down the hall, and as soon as Tessie McGee was given a warning that an intruder was approaching, she would switch and begin teaching from the obligatory text. The teacher and students would collaborate in this subversive type of education.

What a significant history to be elevating at this time!

Yes, our students have been really excited to read about this fugitive pedagogy and discuss the ways that our ancestors have disrupted and transgressed white attempts to limit education for us and to weaponise education to limit us. From those ancestors we learn that education for Black people has *always* been transgressive and focused on liberation and power for our people. And many times it has involved concealment.

That seems particularly pertinent now. I believe it was just last week that schools and universities across the US received a letter that barred schools and colleges from "using race in decisions pertaining to admissions, hiring, promotion, compensation, financial aid, scholarships, prizes, administrative support, discipline, housing, graduation ceremonies and all other aspects of student, academic and campus life" (see Graef & D'Antonio, 2025).

Yes, we received that letter, and all those ultimatums you mentioned are supposedly to "protect" white students against being discriminated against. As the university leadership grapples with how to respond to this letter, we asked our students to analyse it through the lens of fugitive pedagogy. Is this a time to submit and give up? Or do we seek to learn from our ancestors? Do we think about the ways they had to teach children in the 1920s, in the 1930s, when it was illegal to teach about Black people and when there were very real repercussions if the histories of Black resistance were taught.

There are many things we can learn from the history of fugitive pedagogies. The teachers in the 1920s and 1930s found ways to teach subversively, and they didn't do this individually. One of the things I learnt from Jarvis R Givens' (2021) book was how these teachers were networked. They organised nationally, distributed the writings of Carter G Woodson, and would advise colleagues in ways to use these materials to teach Black students. These collective actions were a key element of the art of Black teaching, and this seems one of many things that we can learn from our ancestors as we respond to the challenges of this moment.

The idea of a fugitive pedagogy is, of course, inspired by the actions of the runaway slave who refused to be enslaved. What sort of fugitive pedagogies can we now create that refuse to be enslaved by MAGA fascism or white supremacy and that will transgress and resist the policies and laws they may try to enact?

I find it very moving to think about you and your students turning to and creating fugitive pedagogies at this time. I will be reading that book! This sounds like yet another way in which you are turning to history and ancestry to respond to these current crises. I know that you are also committed to international exchanges as part of a liberative pedagogy. Can you say more about this?

This past summer I took 20 students to South Africa with Professor Toivo Ashekee, who is a brilliant young scholar. This was a study abroad course called "Race, class and gender in contemporary South Africa". It was significant to be there right in the midst of the national elections 30 years after the end of Apartheid. The students were most interested in meeting young South Africans on university campuses. In Cape Town, they engaged with young South Africans who had established a tent city on their campus in solidarity with the Palestinian people who were experiencing genocidal violence in Gaza at the hands of the Israeli military. Our students shared experiences and stories about their own activism and brainstormed ideas for future collaborations. These sorts of Pan-African and internationalist anti-colonial networks are growing among students on campuses.

Currently, it might seem quiet on US campuses because the government is issuing threats and passing laws that are creating great uncertainty for so many people. Now is time to recalibrate, but I believe that our young people are soon to develop new tactics and new forms of resistance on school campuses.

I have two images in my mind as we draw this conversation to a close. One is picturing your students in Pan-African conversations in a tent city in Cape Town. And the other relates to the conversations you are sharing in your classrooms about fugitive pedagogies, these more a conversation with the past, with the work of Carter G Woodson and teachers like Tessie McGee.

Both those experiences were significant to me. It was heartening to listen in on conversations between our students and those in South Africa and to imagine their future collaborations. And it meant a great deal to me to see the passion and commitment of students discussing the histories of fugitive pedagogies. As future scholars and teachers, I wonder how they will carry on those legacies and how they will prepare our next generation to discover its mission and to fulfil it.

Note

[1] Julian Vasquez Heilig described this eloquently and related it to what is taking place in the USA in an interview on *Democracy Now* on 21 February 2025. It can be viewed at https://www.democracynow.org/2025/2/21/schools_trump

References

Givens. J. R. (2021). *Fugitive pedagogy: Carter G. Woodson and the art of Black teaching.* Harvard University Press.

Graef, A., & D'Antonio, I. (2025, February 17). *Education Department letter threatens federal funding of any school that considers race in most aspects of student life.* CNN. https://edition.cnn.com/2025/02/16/politics/education-department-race-federal-funding/index.html

Part five:
Black religion, resistance and revolutionary spirituality

*Black religion, resistance
and revolutionary spirituality*

The two interviews that conclude this book explore realms of Black religion, resistance and revolutionary spirituality. In these disturbing times, and always, spiritual and political practice are interwoven.

16.
For future generations: Spiritual, religious and political practice

David Denborough: I know that your spiritual and religious practice is interwoven with your political and healing work. Can you tell us more about your spiritual and religious history?

Makungu Akinyela: I was born into and grew up within the African Methodist Episcopal Church. I grew up initially in the south, so by the time I got old enough to be aware of the church, my parents were organisers in the civil rights movement, and the church was very important for them. A lot of meetings were held there, a lot of demonstrations and actions were planned in there, and of course, the church was also our place of worship. The African Methodist Episcopal Church is the only church I've ever known, and because of its history of social action for the last 200 years, this shaped a lot of the ways that I've thought about Christianity. I was active in the church until I was about 16 when I got very involved in political activities. This was in the late 1960s, and a lot of the political activities and political actions were very critical of religious people. We were young people looking for direct action and influenced by revolutionary movements around the world. So around that time, I pulled away from the church for a number of years.

I wouldn't call this a crisis of faith; I was just like most young people from my generation. We were very critical of the church because, for the most part, it was promoting a kind of a go-slow, be very patient idea of change, whereas most young people from my generation were looking for revolutionary change. So much so that we sometimes overlooked the things that had been done, but we were looking at what we saw as necessary at that point in history. So we pulled away from participation in religion—we didn't feel that we could get things done through the church at that moment, and I was probably one of millions of young people in the mid- to late-60s and early 1970s in Black communities who began to do political work outside of the church structure. This was a new thing, you know, because for so long the church had been the main institution in our community. In the 1960s and 1970s, other organisations were formed, through which we could do the political work, much more radical work, without being influenced by our parents and church traditions.

Could you say a little bit more about the African Methodist Episcopal Church in African American community and history?

Our church was founded out of resistance to racism and a struggle for social justice by Black people in the north who were for the most part free Black people; they weren't enslaved people. In the north of the United States, they initially had what they called the Free African Society. These were self-care societies that made sure that people were fed, that took care of the dead, and if someone was sick, made sure their families were taken care of. During this time, they participated religiously in different churches, both the Methodist and Episcopalian (Anglican).

A particular group, led by the first bishop of our church, Richard Allen, had gone to pray at a Methodist church in Philadelphia, and they were told that they could not pray at the altar while white people were there, that they had to pray in the balcony, that they weren't allowed to kneel at the altar. But they refused to move until they finished praying. And then once they finished praying, they walked out. They staged a massive walkout of all the Africans, and they never came back. Instead, they formed their own church.

One of their members was a blacksmith, and they began meeting in the blacksmith shop, so the symbol of our church is a blacksmith's anvil. From that time, they formed what they called the African Methodist Episcopal Church. They knew that they were Africans, and so they named the church after themselves. Bishop Allen argued that the basic ideas of Methodism best suited the needs of Africans at that time. Methodism allowed the freedom of worship that Africans needed, but also it allowed an organisation and a discipline. And the church began to build from that time.

It was always at the forefront of the anti-slavery movement. The church supported abolitionists, campaigned against slavery in the south, and it was the first church in North America to make it illegal for any member of the congregation to own slaves. The church also supported slave insurrections—several of their bishops and ministers were involved in giving support to slave insurrections and runaways. The foundation of this church was social justice, and that's always remained a very important part of it. By the 20th century, it grew internationally. South Africa was the first area of Africa in which the African Methodist Episcopal Church was established; it's now also in West Africa and some other parts. These days there are even a couple of African Methodist Episcopal Churches in Europe.

Can you also say something about how Christianity more generally has been important to many African people in America?

The first Africans in North America, the United States, were not Christian in any significant numbers until around the last part of the 18th century. Around the 1790s, there was what was called the great revival. But until that time, during 200 to 300 years of the enslavement period, Africans were not drawn to Christianity in the United States. The first wave of African Christians was after 1790. This was when Africans began to choose to become Christian. And that was because the approach of the great revival was very different from the liturgical churches that had previously dominated church life in North America—the Anglican and Catholic churches, which were based on catechism and readings. In fact,

Christianity didn't impact many white people in North America in the early colonies. There were many missionaries from Europe, from England, and they complained that the settlers didn't seem to have any concern for God, they just wanted to make money! But after 1790, a new style of charismatic worship emerged that was based in orality—preaching. This emotional preaching and storytelling drew a lot of white people. Around this time, the churches would hold big meetings, and at times the slave owners would enable enslaved people to attend. Because of the storytelling style, because it wasn't based in literature but in storytelling, for the first time African people could hear the stories of the Bible. The story of the Hebrews' separation from Egypt was particularly meaningful as this was a central part of enslaved African theology. But then the story of Jesus was also very important because here was a suffering saviour, a God who could identify with your struggle and with what you've been through. This was important for people.

So between 1790 and 1840, significant numbers of African people began to become Christian, and to develop a uniquely African Christianity that appropriated the stories of the Bible and made them meaningful to enslaved people. The stories of liberation within the Bible began to speak directly to Africans in North America. And they were also able to take traditional African ideas and beliefs and African spirituality and ways of worship that did not separate the secular from the sacred. The Christianity that they developed provided room for these forms of worship; that's what Richard Allen meant about Methodism or Christianity allowing a freedom of spirit, a freedom of worship, which Africans needed. But he also believed that you needed a structured discipline, a method, the Wesleyan method.

But I think it was the stories of liberation that have been so significant to Africans in this continent. Throughout the scriptures there are stories of liberation. Stories of God taking the side of the weak and the oppressed and walking with them, whether it's through the Red Sea or whether it's the people who Jesus chose to side with through the Gospels. Africans could hear these stories, and they understood these stories to be important. I think that was really at the bottom of it. This was a kind of theology that gave people hope to hold on and to hold out, as we would say, that there would be something different and better coming through an act of faith. This was a faith not just in prayer but in what we call "walking in that faith", being in it.

Can we come back now to the 1960s, 1970s, when you were heavily involved in political work and had stepped outside the church as the place for action. I remember you saying yesterday that at this time you were reading radical texts and theory rather than religious or Christian writings. Can you just say a little bit about what then brought you back and made you move back towards the church as one forum, not the only forum, but as one forum to continue the struggle?

In some ways, what brought me back to the church is also what initially got me interested in being a therapist. When I was in college, I read Frantz Fanon's *Wretched of the Earth* (1963), and while I didn't understand most of it then, I understood that he was concerned with the mental health of people who were struggling against colonialism. For some reason, that stuck with me, inspired me: the idea that there was healing work that could be done for people who were actually engaged in activism. I had seen that within our movement, concern for mental health was really lacking, and people were getting burnt out.

This was the time of the Black Power movement, and my generation of activists were facing real terrorism. When we went into this struggle, we were inspired by everything else that was happening around the world. Many of us who came from the south, like I did, had come from the civil rights movement, and even though we talked about fascism and oppression, many of us never imagined what the US government would do to protect its own interest.

After years in the struggle, when our people ended up dying, or being arrested, being subject to terrorism from the police, going to jail, facing the murder campaigns from the FBI, I saw a lot of people being burnt out.

At this time when I saw a lot of people in crises, I was married, with small children, and just all kinds of crazy things were happening.

I can remember at one point my wife went to a political meeting, and the people who she was with were surrounded by a troop of FBI agents and police. They all had guns pulled on them and they came close to death. Those kinds of political stresses also create personal stresses, family stresses. It's very difficult to hold a family together and really honour love and marriage when you're also struggling against the state and you have nothing else to give meaning to your world.

Our movement at the time relied a lot on revolutionary theories greatly influenced by European ideas, including Marxism, which were devoid of any reliance on God or understandings of spirituality. In fact, these theories ridiculed spirituality and the church. A lot of people from our generation were trying to wage a political struggle in so-called materialist ways, to use a Marxist term. We didn't necessarily consider ourselves Marxist, but we were very much influenced by the spirit of that period and those ways of thinking about waging revolution.

Sometimes, however, this leads to a fantasy world in which the revolution is everything. But revolution is not the end of the world; there must be a vision and a dream beyond the revolution or else it can become very empty. I think that's what I experienced.

Without a spiritual centre, without a reliance on something greater than yourself, people had nowhere else to go, you hit bottom and that's it. Some people began to rely on drugs, alcohol. When soldiers came back from Vietnam, they called it post-traumatic stress disorder. Well many of the young people from the Black Power movement suffered something similar, but they had no veterans' association or veterans' hospital. I saw a lot of people being burnt out, and it seemed there was only so far you can go on human energy. Traditionally, our communities are organised around our churches, and traditionally there's no division between secular and sacred.

It was very good that I had my family, my parents who—as critical as I was of their church, which to me was not doing enough, was not committed enough to waging a real struggle for self-determination and human rights—my parents were always who I would call. They were like true Christians. They never closed the doors even when we had conflicts, and they were always very supportive of what I did. They didn't agree, they didn't like a lot of it [laughs], but they were always there. And so, at the bottom, at that point when I was feeling total frustration, what I had was my mother and my father who would say, "here, look, try this".

And there was a church in our city—I was in California at that time— which was pastored by a man who was very much involved with liberation theology. A lot of people who had been politically active and had nowhere else to go began going there, and they were able to hear a gospel that made sense in the context of social justice and political change. It was an African Methodist Episcopal Church. Besides hearing the gospel that made fighting for freedom okay, being there also reconnected me with those old traditions. I was hearing songs that I hadn't heard for a very long time, and this began to reknit the meaning of a world for me. I think tradition is very important, traditional rituals are very important.

In my generation, one of the things that we had taken from the spirit of international revolutionary change was that we were often throwing tradition aside. Like the so-called Cultural Revolution in China where people tried to throw away tradition. But I began to rethink this and to see that new change has to come out of what's in the tradition. I began to see in a new light the importance of the traditions of my ancestors, and I also saw the importance of honouring the struggles that they did and the way they did it. Even though we didn't always continue it in the same way, really honouring those things is important. And this included honouring the connection to God and the dependence on God to strengthen us to carry on our struggle.

For me, this was an important personal discovery. I have also come to believe that a movement needs to be connected to something greater than itself. It's not enough just to get social justice, to get political power, because if that power is not guided by something greater than the individuals who wield the power, it can very easily get corrupted.

At the same time, I realised long ago that you can't depend on a church to change the world. Whereas when I was younger, I expected the church to absolutely follow our radical politics, as I got a little older, the words of Black theologian Gayraud Wilmore spoke to me. He wrote a book called

Black Religion and Black Radicalism (1973), and in it he says that the Black church is always the most revolutionary and the most reactionary institution in the Black community at the same time, and it's that tension that creates and sustains us. The church is an important part of us, of who we are as a people.

Can I ask how these spiritual considerations influence you in the counselling room?

At the heart of my spiritual practice and religious practice are concerns about ethics. These are considerations about how you live your life. I do believe that there is something greater or more than myself. I do believe that life goes on after us and that this creates an ethical requirement. I believe that the way I live my life on this side of the door also creates what my life will be like on the other side of the door. This brings me an ethical requirement to think about the real effects of what I do, whether I'm teaching or practising.

This way of thinking shapes the whole notion of therapy for me. When people come to me, I think we're looking for ways to help them to meet their own ethical requirements of life. I don't work in a religious setting, and I'm not a pastoral counsellor, but my own spirituality guides me. I don't make a distinction between who I am spiritually and who I am in the professional world; there's no secular/sacred divide for me. It's all just one piece.

I've also heard you talk about the ethical requirements in relation to seeking to be an ancestor. I guess this relates to African spiritualities ...

Yes, ancestorship is not guaranteed. The ancestors are the righteous dead. In Yoruba culture in West Africa, the term *iwa pele* is used for "good character". Our whole purpose in life is to learn good character, develop good character. My grandmother would call this to be a righteous person, to be a good Christian. But in Yoruba culture, *iwa pele* is what we seek to do. That's the purpose of our life. We come to the marketplace, the earth, and in the marketplace, we engage with different lessons and experiences in life, and those experiences are to teach us to have *iwa pele*. If at the end of our life we have had *iwa pele*, good character, when we die, we are remembered by those who still live: our children, our grandchildren.

So to become an ancestor, it's not enough just to live and die. You have to live with *iwa pele*, and we seek to do this so that when we die, people will venerate you as an ancestor, they will remember your name, they will offer you libations and prayers, give you water offerings and drink offerings and call your name at every family gathering.

And no matter who else is there in the family, the ancestors are always there. When we have a gathering, when we have a party, when we have a religious ceremony, the ancestors are invited in to be a part of that. But if no one calls your name, you actually no longer live.

The great Kenyan religious scholar John Mbiti (1985) said that the ancestors are the living dead. They're not really dead. They're living. They're living in a different realm. But when people stop calling your name, then you're truly dead. This cosmology sets up a relationship of ethics. Parents, adults, want to treat children well because they want to be remembered and respected by those children when they become elders. And we say that when elders die, they are going to the place where children just came from. Children are taught to respect elders. And the elders are required to live a good life to become ancestors. This is all to create ethical relationships within community.

And are there ways in which this sense of spirituality and ethical ancestorship relates to revolutionary politics and action?

To answer that question, I think it's best to turn to the words of Assata Shakur who, in a conversation I shared with her in Cuba, spoke about her spirituality being linked to her grandmother's dreams and also how it has involved deliberate decisions.

Assata: For me, becoming spiritual has been a process and also a decision. Deciding whether to go through this life alone or going through this life with my ancestors, with my friends, with my spiritual ancestors, with all that energy. I take in good energy and I'd prefer to go through life like that. I do not prefer to go through life alone.

Makungu: So your spirituality is an act of choice. It's a decision.

Assata: In part, yeah. It's also an important thing to always understand, to recognise, that wherever you are, you didn't do it alone; you didn't come here alone and that means that you have debt, you have responsibility. You have to pay homage to all those people that worked to get you wherever you were, whether they're your momma, whether they're, maybe, out of the street that minded you when you were five. You know, you have a debt for all you know, not only to people that helped you, not only to ancestors, because of debt for what you know, the more you know, the more you owe. I never thought of it like that before, but I like that, "the more you know the more you owe".

That sounds like a powerful spiritual and political commitment.

Yes. Our ancestors over the last 400 years at times didn't know if they could survive, didn't know if they could make it, but because of their ancestors, because of the experience of the spirit in their lives, they were able to hold on. And because they held on, we are able to be here. It's only because our ancestors could hold on that we are here. So now it's our work to hold on despite the hard times for those who come after us, for the next generation.

References

Fanon, F. (1963). *The wretched of the earth.* Grove.
Mbiti, J. S. (1985). *African religions and philosophy.* Heinemann.
Wilmore, G. S. (1973). *Black religion and Black radicalism: An examination of the Black experience in religion.* Anchor.

17. Let us march on

David Denborough: I find that interview, "For future generations: Spiritual, religious and political practice", invigorating. And I remember speaking with you as we sat in Martinique, looking out at that ocean that Frantz Fanon would have viewed and perhaps swam in as a child. Since that conversation in Martinique, white Christian nationalism is now exerting its influence over so many aspects of American life and beyond US borders to places such as East Africa in relation to LGBTQ lives. It is a very particular version of a violent racist Christianity that is a key force in authoritarian developments in the USA. I know you grew up in Mississippi, perhaps the birthplace many decades ago of white Christian ethno-nationalism (Ku Klux Klan) in the USA. Over your lifetime you've seen the horrors that such forms of Christianity unleash. At the same time, you described in the previous interview how Africans in the USA have drawn on Black religion and spirituality across 400 years to sustain and make possible many generations of struggle. At this particular time in history, what is the role of liberatory theology, Black theology and church community for you?

Makungu Akinyela: You're quite right to name how a particular version of a violent, racist Christianity is a major force in helping this kind of authoritarian movement that's come up in America right now. It's a central influence. And, as you say, those harmful and hurtful ideas are also being spread internationally including into East Africa in ways that further weaken Africa in a continuing colonial way.

And yet, there is resistance. As MAGA fascism in the guise of evangelical Christianity seeks to dominate this society, there is a radical response occurring within Black churches to reclaim a liberatory tradition as first defined by Dr James Cone in his book *A Black Theology of Liberation* (1970/2010), which he wrote in 1970 and people are rereading now. Also influential are Black preachers in the prophetic tradition like elder statesman Rev Jeremiah Wright and awesome Black womanist prophetic preacher Rev Renita Weems. I think also of Bishop William Barber who has been leading the Poor People's Campaign and Moral Mondays and challenging state policies against workers and poor people particularly in the south. And then there is Bible scholar Dr Obery Hendricks Jr. who is the author of illuminating books *Christians against Christianity* (2021) and *The Politics of Jesus* (2006). And this is just within the Christian tradition of which I am a part.

As I described in the earlier interview, African American religious experience is a collaboration of traditional African spirituality, Muslim influence as well as Christian traditions both from the West and from Indigenous African Christianity. The unique experience of resisting white racism and enslavement in the USA has shaped our religious tradition and continues to.

Alongside your grassroots community organising and teaching and therapeutic practice, you are also a minister within the African Methodist Episcopal Church. When you stand in front of your congregation in these times, what are you drawing on as you speak with them, as you sing with them?

When I am speaking in church, as part of the ritual of service, it's important to me to link whatever I am saying to the present moment. I try to talk about what this time looks like and to ask, "In this moment, what would the creator call us to be doing if we're being faithful to our religious tradition?" My personal theology and spirituality is based on a belief that the entire Bible, when read from the bottom up and not the top down, is anti-imperialist. From the story of the Tower of Babel, which was about the crumbling down of an attempt to build an empire; to the Hebrew resistance to enslavement in Kemet Egypt, which was an empire of that time; to the struggle of Jewish people during the Babylonian empire; to the descriptions of the Roman Empire and all the work of Jesus; to me the entire spectrum of the Bible is anti-imperialist. I believe that God has always been against empire, so for me when I ask, "In this moment, what would the creator call us to be doing if we're being faithful to our religious tradition?", it evokes for me an anti-imperialist God. A God who will stand with us as we resist empire and domination.

These times must no doubt be frightening for your congregation, so I can picture the significance of this evocation of a God standing with you. Can you help me also get a sense of the feeling or sound of your church community at this time. I have had the pleasure of visiting your church, so I know there would be singing ...

Oh yes. Every Sunday this month, in Black History Month, you got to open up with the Black national anthem, right? *Lift every voice and sing* is a hymn written as a poem by James Weldon Johnson, who was a principal of a segregated school. He wrote the poem 125 years ago, in 1900. His brother, John Rosamond Johnson, composed the music for the lyrics.

> God of our weary years,
>
> God of our silent tears,
>
> Thou who has brought us thus far on the way;
>
> Thou who has by Thy might
>
> Led us into the light,
>
> Keep us forever in the path, we pray.

This anthem is an appeal to God to lead us back to our homeland, to our Motherland. And when we sing it together, it recognises all that we've been through.

We have come over a way that with tears has been watered,

We have come, treading our path through the blood of the slaughtered.

This song, that just about every Black church recognises, has been the primary song in every service this month. Through it we draw strength.

Lift every voice and sing,

'Til earth and heaven ring,

Ring with the harmonies of Liberty;

Let our rejoicing rise

High as the list'ning skies,

Let it resound loud as the rolling sea.

Sing a song full of the faith that the dark past has taught us,

Sing a song full of the hope that the present has brought us;

Facing the rising sun of our new day begun,

Let us march on 'til victory is won.

(Johnson & Johnson, 1900)

References

Cone, J. (2010). *A Black theology of liberation.* Orbis. (Original work published 1970)

Hendricks, O., Jr. (2006). *The politics of Jesus: Rediscovering the true revolutionary nature of Jesus' teachings and how they have been corrupted.* Doubleday.

Hendricks, O., Jr. (2021). *Christians against Christianity: How right-wing evangelicals are destroying our nation and our faith.* Beacon.

Johnson, J. R., & Johnson, J. W. (1900). *Lift every voice and sing.* Stern.

About the chapters

Some of the chapters in this book have been published previously. Others are original to this volume.

Chapter 1, "Decolonising our lives: Divining a postcolonial therapy", was originally published in *International Journal of Narrative Therapy and Community Work*, 2002(2): 32–43.

Chapter 2, "Testimony of hope: African-centred praxis for therapeutic ends", was originally published in *Journal of Systemic Therapies*, 2005(24/1): 5–18.

Chapter 3, "Decolonised counselling in a time of rising fascism", is from an interview with Makungu Akinyela by David Denborough, conducted online in March 2025.

Chapter 4, "Standing together at the Door of Return" by James Amemasor and Makungu Akinyela, was a speech originally delivered at the International Narrative Therapy and Community Work Conference held at Spelman College in Atlanta, Georgia, USA, on 19 June 2002.

Chapter 5, "Opening the Door of Return", is an interview with James Anani Amemasor. This interview took place in Cape Coast Castle in

Ghana. The interviewers were Cheryl White, Makungu Akinyela and David Denborough. It was originally published in *International Journal of Narrative Therapy and Community Work*, 2002(2): 60–63.

Chapter 6, "Spiritual accountability and balance: A story from the counselling room", is an extract from the paper "Reparations: Repairing relationships and honouring ancestry". This was originally published in *International Journal of Narrative Therapy and Community Work*, 2002(2): 46–49.

Chapter 7, "Connecting with ancestral struggle to strengthen resistance", is from an interview with Makungu Akinyela by David Denborough, conducted online in March 2025.

Chapter 8, "Kujichagulia: Self-determination and the power of names", is from a conversation that took place between Makungu Akinyela and David Denborough in Martinique in August 2023.

Chapter 9, "Rethinking Afrocentricity: The foundation of a theory of critical Africentricity", was originally published in *Culture and difference: Critical perspectives on the bicultural experience in the United States* (edited by Antonia Darder, Praeger, 1995, pp. 21–39).

Chapter 10, "Cabral, Black liberation and cultural struggle", was first published in *Claim no easy victories: The legacy of Amilcar Cabral* (edited by Firoze Manji & Bill Fletcher Jr., Daraja Press, 2013, pp. 445–452).

Chapter 11, "Culture is the heartbeat of revolution", is a speech given by Makungu Akinyela for the National Malcolm X Assassination Commemoration in February 2022. It was published in *BAMN: By Any Means Necessary* 2002(4/1): 20–24.

Chapter 12, "Cultural resistance when the house is burning", is from an interview with Makungu Akinyela by David Denborough, conducted online in March 2025.

About the chapters

Chapter 13, "Education as an experience of freedom", has not been published previously.

Chapter 14, "Valuing everyday resistance in Black family life: A story of critical pedagogy from the university of the streets", combines previously unpublished work with an extract from Makungu Akinyela's PhD thesis *Black families, cultural democracy and self-determination: An African-centered pedagogy* (Emory University, 1996).

Chapter 15, "Fugitive pedagogies", is from an interview with Makungu Akinyela by David Denborough, conducted online in March 2025.

Chapter 16, "For future generations: Spiritual, religious and political practice", is a conversation that took place between Makungu Akinyela and David Denborough in Martinique in August 2023.

Chapter 17, "Let us march on", is from an interview with Makungu Akinyela by David Denborough, conducted online in March 2025.

Thank you to the publishers for permission to reprint previously published works in this collection.

Abbreviations

AAABC	Afro-American Anti-Bicentennial Committee
BPPSD	Black Panther Party for Self Defense
CAPA	Coalition Against Police Abuse
DSM	Diagnostic and Statistical Manual of Mental Illnesses (American Psychiatric Association)
HOU	House of Umoja (formerly Black Panther Party of Northern California)
LGBTQ	lesbian, gay, bisexual, trans and queer
MAGA	make America great again (slogan popularised by Donald Trump and used to describe his political platform and followers)
MXGM	Malcolm X Grassroots Movement
NAACP	National Association for the Advancement of Colored People
PTSD	post-traumatic stress disorder
RAM	Revolutionary Action Movement
UNESCO	The United Nations Educational, Scientific and Cultural Organization
UNIA	Universal Negro Improvement Association
VA	Veterans Administration (US Department of Veterans Affairs)

www.ingramcontent.com/pod-product-compliance
Lightning Source LLC
Chambersburg PA
CBHW031150020426
42333CB00013B/596